OCCUPIED
EAST JERUSALEM

Editors
Hady Matar, Assistant Program Director, Palestine Works
Omar Yousef Shehabi, Executive Director, Palestine Works

Contributors

Emma Herman, BA candidate, 2017, University of Chicago
Samar Khan, JD candidate, 2017, New York University
Anjali Manivannan, JD, New York University
Alice McBurney, LLB (Hons), Australian National University
Asma Peracha, JD candidate, 2017, New York University
Justin Schwegel, JD, Georgetown University
Anan Abu Shanab, MSc, University of Oxford

ISBN 978-0692476840
Published by Palestine Works Inc.
1200 18th Street NW, Suite 700
Washington, District of Columbia 20036
United States of America

TABLE OF CONTENTS

I. Introduction

Israel's policies and practices within occupied East Jerusalem (oEJ) constitute ongoing, systematic and gross violations of international humanitarian law and international human rights law. This is "normal life" for Palestinians in East Jerusalem: an all-encompassing discriminatory policy that maintains the occupation and seeks to forcibly displace the indigenous population from its land. Meanwhile, Israel creates facts on the ground that alter the demographics and character of the city and seek to consolidate permanent Israeli control over the city. Such policies seek to foreclose an end to the occupation in accordance with United Nations Security Council (UNSC) Resolution 242 and general principles of international law.

These Israeli practices of discrimination, dispossession and repression towards Palestinians in East Jerusalem reached extraordinary levels during the military operations conducted in the occupied Palestinian territory (oPt) since 13 June 2014. That day, Israel launched "Operation Brother's Keeper," ostensibly to find and rescue three Israeli settler youths who had gone missing in the West Bank. In reality, the Israeli defense and political establishment, who had evidence that the youths had been killed immediately by their kidnappers, used their recovery as a pretext for a major military offensive in the West Bank. That offensive targeted Hamas, which two weeks earlier had agreed to the formation of a Palestinian national consensus government that would govern the West Bank and Gaza and complete the Palestinian reconciliation process.

Outrage at the kidnapping, war patriotism surrounding Operation Brother's Keeper, and incitement by Israeli officials and public figures combined to unleash a wave of Israeli violence and hate speech against Palestinians. East Jerusalem, as the one place where Israeli civilians come into regular contact with Palestinians from the oPt, was the epicenter of this violence. Israeli officials acknowledged, condoned and even encouraged this violence, while the Israeli Security Forces (ISF) took little or no action to stop it. Israel thereby acknowledged and adopted this private violence, and thus is liable for it under the law of state responsibility.

This wave of violence culminated in the kidnapping and brutal murder of Muhammad Abu Khdeir on 2 July by three Israeli Jewish extremists. Muhammad's killing, coupled with the launch of Israel's "Operation Protective Edge" in the Gaza Strip, which killed nearly 2,200 Palestinians, spawned a wave of demonstrations and protests throughout Palestinian neighborhoods in East Jerusalem. The ISF violently suppressed this protest movement through the use of excessive force, arbitrary and extrajudicial killings, arbitrary arrests and detentions, home invasions, and acts of collective punishment. By employing these practices, Israel violated its obligations under international humanitarian law, human rights law, and international policing standards.

As part of this repression, Israel tightened restrictions on Palestinian cultural and religious practices during this period, which coincided with the Islamic holy month of Ramadan (28 June – 28 July 2014). The Israeli authorities severely restricted Palestinian access to the Al-Aqsa Mosque Compound, including the first total closure of the Compound in 47 years. At the same time, they provoked Palestinian and Muslim sentiments by increasing access for extremist Jewish Israelis to pray at the Compound, a practice which Israel's rabbinical establishment strictly forbids. These extremist Jewish Israelis were escorted at the Compound by a heavy ISF presence. ISF personnel repeatedly used excessive and unjustified force against Palestinians at the Al-Aqsa Compound during the relevant period. These acts occurred against the backdrop of an Israeli political discourse of asserting sovereignty over the Al-Aqsa Compound, exacerbating the cycle of instability.

This report reviews these acts under international human rights law and international humanitarian law. While this report focuses on incidents occurring in the context of the military operations conducted since 13 June 2014, they occurred in the broader context of an Israeli occupation of East Jerusalem that is illegal per se under international humanitarian law and engenders continuous and systematic violations of international human rights law.

I. International Law Framework Governing East Jerusalem

A. Background History

Under the Partition Plan adopted by United Nations General Assembly (UNGA) Resolution 181, Jerusalem was to be placed under international sovereignty. However, violence between the Arab and Jewish communities in Palestine broke out in response to Resolution 181 and the Partition Plan was never instituted. As a result of the 1948 Arab-Israeli War, the newly-declared State of Israel asserted sovereignty over West Jerusalem while Jordan asserted sovereignty over East Jerusalem, defined as a 6.5 km^2 area covering the Old City and its surrounding neighborhoods. Jordan's annexation of the West Bank, including East Jerusalem, was not widely recognized.

In the June 1967 War, Israel occupied the West Bank, including East Jerusalem, and the Gaza Strip. Israel effectively annexed East Jerusalem in June 1967 through the extension of Israeli law and absorbed East Jerusalem into the West Jerusalem municipality. When Israel redrew the boundaries of municipal Jerusalem, it expanded East Jerusalem from 6.5 km^2 to 71 km^2 by absorbing 28 surrounding Palestinian villages. This expanded municipal Jerusalem came under Israeli civil authority, while the rest of the oPt was subject to military rule. Israel purported to formally annex East Jerusalem in 1980 by adopting the Basic Law: Jerusalem, which declares expanded municipal Jerusalem as the capital of Israel.

The UNSC has consistently asserted that that Israel must withdraw from all of the territory it occupied in the 1967 War, including East Jerusalem.[1]

B. Israel's Illegal Occupation and Annexation of East Jerusalem

1. Occupation

The Israeli occupation of East Jerusalem is illegal because it violates the three fundamental principles underlying the law of occupation. First, an occupying power does not have sovereignty or title in an occupied territory. Secondly, occupation is a form of trust, administered for the benefit of the occupied population in a way that is consistent with the restoration of their right to self-determination. Thirdly, as a consequence of these two principles, occupation must be temporary. A growing body of scholarship recognizes that an occupation that violates these principles is per se illegal.[2]

---

1 UNSC Res. 242 (1967), Res. 338 (1973).

a. Occupation does not confer sovereignty

Occupation is an abnormal condition in the international order insofar as it suspends the sovereign equality of States. The nonsovereignty of occupation derives from the UN Charter principle that territory cannot be acquired, and sovereignty cannot be lost, through the use of force. It is bolstered by the understanding in modern international law that sovereignty over occupied territory is vested in the population under occupation rather than in the ousted sovereign.

Israel plainly asserts that it is the lawful sovereign over oEJ. Its 1980 Basic Law: Jerusalem declares all of Israeli-defined municipal Jerusalem, including East Jerusalem, as the capital of Israel. A 2000 amendment prohibits the transfer of any part of municipal Jerusalem to any "foreign body," such as the Palestinian government or an international organization. Shortly after the Basic Law: Jerusalem was adopted, UNSC Resolution 478 resolved that all legislative measures and action taken by Israel that alter or purport to alter the character and status of Jerusalem are null and void.

b. Occupation is a form of trust

Occupation is also an abnormal condition in the international order because it suspends the occupied population's exercise of its right to self-determination. The requirement that foreign administration of territory must comply with principles of trust has been recognized since the establishment of the Mandate system, which resolved that the Mandated powers bore a "sacred trust of civilization" to facilitate the self-determination of the peoples of the Mandated territories.[3]

This understanding of foreign administration as a trusteeship was at the heart of the International Court of Justice's (ICJ) 1971 Namibia advisory opinion, which affirmed the UNGA's revocation of South Africa's mandate

---

2 See, e.g., Orna Ben-Naftali, Aeyal M. Gross, and Keren Michaeli, Illegal Occupation: Framing the Occupied Palestinian Territory, 23 Berkeley J. Int'l L. 551 (2005); Legal Consequences of the Construction of a Wall in the Occupied Palestinian Territory, Advisory Opinion, [2004] ICJ Rep 136 (July 9, 2004) [hereinafter "Legal Consequences of a Wall"], Separate Opinion of Judge Elaraby; Antonio Cassese, Self-Determination: A Legal Reprisal (1995); Richard Falk and Burns Weston, "The Relevance of International Law to Israeli and Palestinian Rights in the West Bank and Gaza," in International Law and the Administration of Occupied Territories (Playfair, ed., 1992) pp. 146-147.

3 League of Nations Covenant art. 22.

for Namibia.[4] The Court held that South Africa's infringement on the rights and welfare of the Namibian people through apartheid rule destroyed the object and purpose of the "sacred trust" and thus rendered South Africa's continued presence in Namibia an illegal foreign occupation.[5]

In the case of occupation, the occupying power bears an obligation to administer the territory in the best interests of the occupied population until its self-determination can be restored through a political settlement.

Israel's policies of dispossession and discrimination against Palestinians in the oPt violates this trust. Israel administers the West Bank, including oEJ, for the benefit of its illegal settler population through a pervasive regime of institutional discrimination between settlers and Palestinians that is widely recognized as apartheid.[6] As detailed herein, Israel's overarching policy aim in oEJ is to expand the Jewish presence and character of the city by increasing the illegal Israeli settler population while marginalizing the Palestinian population and Arab character of the city through acts of individual and collective dispossession. Such an overarching policy of population transfer of the indigenous population clearly violates the trusteeship obligation.

c. Occupation must be temporary

Occupation, as the suspension of sovereign equality and self-determination, must be temporary. In sanctioning wide-ranging changes to the laws, institutions and physical character of the oPt, including East Jerusalem, the Israeli Supreme Court has taken the position that while

---

4 Legal Consequences for States of the Continued Presence of South Africa in Namibia (South West Africa) notwithstanding Security Council Resolution 276 (1970), Advisory Opinion, [1971] ICJ Rep 16 [hereinafter "Namibia (South West Africa)"].

5 Id. at ¶ 53 ("the ultimate objective of the sacred trust was the self-determination and independence of the people's concerned") and ¶ 95 ("By stressing that South Africa 'has, in fact, disavowed the Mandate', the General Assembly declared in fact that it had repudiated it. The resolution in question is therefore to be viewed as the exercise of the right to terminate a relationship in case of a deliberate and persistent violation of obligations which destroys the very object and purpose of that relationship.")

6 See, e.g., Report of the Special Rapporteur on the situation of human rights in the Palestinian territories occupied since 1967, Richard Falk, A/HRC/25/67 (Jan. 13, 2014), ¶¶ 51-77; Report of the Special Rapporteur on the situation of human rights in the Palestinian territories occupied since 1967, John Dugard, A/HRC/4/17 (Jan. 29, 2007), ¶¶ 49-50, 58-63; John Dugard and John Reynolds, Apartheid, International Law, and the Occupied Palestinian Territory', European Journal of International Law 24, 3 (2013); Russell Tribunal on Palestine, Findings of the Final Session (Mar. 16-17, 2013),§ 2; Beyond Occupation Apartheid, Colonialism and International Law in the Occupied Palestinian Territories (Virginia Tilley, ed., 2012).

occupation cannot be permanent, it may continue indefinitely.[7] This position is untenable because it nullifies "the interest of the occupied people to … regain control of their lives and exercise their right to self-determination, and the interest of the international community in resuming the normal order of sovereign equality between states."[8] Thus, an indefinite occupation is an illegal occupation.

Israel's indefinite occupation of the oPt, in particular its supposedly permanent annexation of East Jerusalem, violates the temporary nature of occupation. Its Basic Law: Jerusalem states that the entire unified municipality will forever remain its undivided capital. No senior Israeli government official has ever claimed otherwise, nor has any government been willing to engage in serious final-status negotiations that would end the occupation of East Jerusalem in conformity with UNSC Resolution 242. Moreover, the settlements, industrial zones, settler road networks, and major infrastructure projects demonstrate the permanence of Israel's designs for East Jerusalem.

2. **Annexation**

In 1967, the Israeli government redrew the municipal boundaries of its West Jerusalem municipality to absorb all of what had historically been considered Jerusalem, including the Old City and the immediately surrounding neighborhoods. The new municipality also included Palestinian areas that were historically considered villages outside Jerusalem, such as Beit Hanina, Shuafat, and Kafr Aqab. It provided the residents of this new Jerusalem municipality with "permanent residency" status in Israel. Palestinians in the remainder of the West Bank received a separate legal status that restricted their lives to certain areas in the oPt, excluding East Jerusalem. These Palestinians are prohibited from entering Israeli-defined Jerusalem without a military permit.

Israel de facto annexed this expanded East Jerusalem in 1967 when it extended Israeli law to oEJ and began administering municipal Jerusalem as a single administrative unit. It de jure annexed East Jerusalem in

7 See Meir Shamgar, "Legal Concepts and Problems of the Israeli Military Government-The Initial Stage", in Military Government in the Territories Administered by Israel: 1967-1980 (1982) at 43. Shamgar was a judge on the Israel Supreme Court from 1975 to 1995 and the Court's President from 1983.

8 Ben-Naftali et al., Illegal Occupation, supra n. 2, at 599.

1980 by adopting the quasi-constitutional Basic Law: Jerusalem, which declares the Jerusalem municipality as Israel's "undivided and eternal" capital. The annexation violates Article 2(4) of the United Nations Charter, which forbids the acquisition and aggrandizement of territory by force. Immediately following the 1980 annexation, UNSC Resolution 478 declared that Israel's annexation was illegal. the UNSC has adopted numerous resolutions declaring that any attempts by Israel to change the status of oEJ are null and void.[9]

C. Israel's Occupation Constitutes a Denial of Palestinian Self-Determination

The International Court of Justice (ICJ) held in its 2004 advisory opinion that Israel's construction of a wall in occupied Palestinian territory, which gives effect to illegal Israeli settlements in and around East Jerusalem by placing the vast majority of oEJ on the "Israeli side" of the wall, constitutes a breach of Israel's obligation to respect the Palestinian people's right of self-determination.[10]

The ICJ decision dealt only with the legal consequences of the construction of the wall. Since 1967, Palestinian land has been annexed and placed under a foreign entity's governing control. The Palestinians are subject to the legal regime of a foreign power that criminalizes and penalizes various expressions of Palestinian self-determination. The Palestinian population has virtually no real control over electing and choosing the leaders. There is no functional ability to effect a democratic and non-violent change in the leadership or the laws.

Moreover, East Jerusalem, which is the economic, social and cultural capital of the Palestinian people, has been effectively severed from the remainder of the oPt, including the West Bank. Thus, the Israeli annexation of East Jerusalem has wide-ranging effects on Palestinians throughout the oPt. Israeli acts to consolidate the separation of East Jerusalem from the rest of the West Bank violate not only international humanitarian law, but Israel's commitment in the Oslo Accords to recognize the West Bank,

---

9 See, e.g., UNSC Res. 252 (1968); Res. 267 (1969): Res. 298 (1971); Res. 476 (1980); Res. 478 (1980).

10 Legal Consequences of a Wall, supra n. 2, at ¶ 122.

including East Jerusalem, and the Gaza Strip as a single territorial unit, the integrity of which would be preserved pending final-status negotiations.[11]

D. Status of Palestinians in East Jerusalem

When Israel de facto annexed East Jerusalem in 1967, it gave Palestinians in oEJ a legal status distinct from that of other Palestinians in the oPt. Palestinians outside oEJ were granted permanent residency within the West Bank and Gaza Strip and came under Israeli military jurisdiction. In contrast, Palestinians within the new Israeli-drawn municipality of Jerusalem were granted what is colloquially known as "Jerusalem IDs." This amounts to a permanent residency status within Israel, including municipal Jerusalem. Non-citizen residents who are not covered by the 1950 Law of Return (i.e. non-Jews) and Syrians in the occupied Golan Heights have the same status. Thus, Palestinians in oEJ, the indigenous population who fell under Israeli control in 1967, are treated as non-Jewish "immigrants" to Israel.

Palestinians in oEJ must consistently prove that their center of life is within municipal Jerusalem. If Jerusalem ID holders are unable to prove to the Israeli Ministry of Interior that their center of life is in Jerusalem, they are at risk of having their residency revoked. Since 1967, Israel has revoked the Jerusalem residency rights of over 14,000 Palestinians, and many thousands are more are at risk of revocation. Indeed, revocation of Jerusalem residency rights is one of Israel's primary methods of forcibly "transferring" Palestinians from oEJ.

While Jerusalem permanent residents may apply for Israeli citizenship, most Palestinians in oEJ reject citizenship as acquiescence to Israeli claims of sovereignty over East Jerusalem. As such, Jerusalemites taking Israeli citizenship is a taboo act within Palestinian circles. However, for those Palestinians who do apply, the process is difficult and requires them to swear an oath of loyalty to Israel, which violates IHL.[12] Moreover, it

---

11 Israel-PLO Declaration of Principles on Interim Self-Governing Arrangements, 32 I.L.M. 1525 (1993) [hereinafter "Israel-PLO Declaration of Principles"] art. IV.

12 Convention (IV) respecting the Laws and Customs of War on Land and its Annex: Regulations concerning the Laws and Customs of War on Land, Oct. 18, 1907 [hereinafter "Hague Regulations"], art. 45 ("It is forbidden to compel the inhabitants of occupied territory to swear allegiance to the hostile Power.")

is not available to Palestinians convicted of security offenses, and often times, to Palestinians who have an immediate family member that has been convicted of a security offense.

Unlike the Palestinians in other parts of the oPt, Palestinians with a Jerusalem ID are subject to Israeli civil law rather than military law.[13] Theoretically, this is the same law to which Jewish Israelis, including settlers, are subject. However, the law is institutionally and systematically designed to subjugate Palestinians. Moreover, in practice, the law is applied discriminatorily. For example, while both Palestinians and Jewish-Israelis are required to receive building permits for home construction in East Jerusalem, the municipality very rarely grants these permits for Palestinians. Moreover, the Israeli response to homes built without a permit by Palestinians in East Jerusalem is disproportionate to the government's response to homes built illegally by Jewish-Israelis. The Palestinian homes are often demolished with no compensation, while this rarely happens to Jewish-Israelis homes. For example, settler outposts in the West Bank, which are illegal even under Israeli law, are rarely actually demolished notwithstanding pending demolition orders against it, and often time are retroactively legalized, becoming a government-sponsored settlement.

E. Applicable Law

According to UN Human Rights Council Resolution S-21, this Commission's mandate includes "all violations of international humanitarian law and international human rights law..." In 2004, the International Court of Justice affirmatively ruled on what bodies of law are applicable to the occupied Palestinian territories, including East Jerusalem.

1. International Humanitarian Law (IHL)

According to the 2004 ICJ Opinion on the Legality of the Wall in Occupied Palestinian Territory, the following rules and provisions of international humanitarian law are applicable:

- The Hague Regulations, which are binding on Israel as

13 However, Jerusalem ID holders are subject to military jurisdiction if they are present in the oPt or if they are accused of an offense deemed to have a connection with the oPt, notwithstanding that they are subject to concurrent Israel civil jurisdiction. See Defence (Emergency) Regulations, 1945, art. 15.

a matter of customary international law.[14]

- Geneva Convention (IV), which Israel and Jordan ratified in 1951.[15] Although Israel disputes the applicability of Geneva Convention (IV) to the West Bank, including East Jerusalem, numerous United Nations Security Council resolutions and the 2004 ICJ advisory opinion establish its applicability.[16]

2. International Human Rights Law (IHRL)

According to the 2004 ICJ advisory opinion, international human rights treaties are applicable within the oPt. This includes the International Covenant on Civil and Political Rights, and the International Covenant on Economic, Social and Cultural Rights. The court held that even though the oPt was outside of Israel's national territory, IHRL was still applicable because the oPt was under Israel's jurisdiction.[17]

While the Oslo Accords identify the status of Jerusalem as an issue for final-status negotiations[18], the Palestinian Authority (PA) does not exercise any authority within East Jerusalem during the interim period established by the Accords. While the Oslo Accords provide for the interim period to end by 1999, it continues until the present day because no final-status agreement has been concluded. Moreover, Israel has outlawed through its own domestic legislation any Palestinian Authority activity within Jerusalem without prior Israeli approval. In short, the PA plays no role in the administration of occupied East Jerusalem, and maintains no jurisdiction

---

14 Hague Regulations, supra n. 12; Construction of a Wall, supra n. 2, at ¶ 89 (observing that Hague Regulations are binding on Israel as customary international law).

15 Geneva Convention (IV) relative to the protection of civilian persons in time of war, 75 UNTS 973, art 4.

16 For UNSC resolutions establishing the applicability of Geneva Convention (IV) to the oPt, see, e.g., UNSC Res. 446 (1979), Res. 471 (1980), Res 607 (1988).

17 Israel argues that the human rights treaties to which it is a party only apply to the territory over which it claims sovereignty. It further argues that most West Bank Palestinians live in "Area A", under the jurisdiction of the Palestinian Authority, and thus that Israel is not responsible for implementing the treaty in those areas. The UN Human Rights Committee and other UN human rights treaty bodies have consistently held that Israel's human rights treaty obligations extend to the oPt in its entirety. See, e.g., UN Human Rights Committee, Concluding Observations on the fourth periodic report on Israel, UN Doc. No. CCPR/C/ISR/CO/4 (Nov. 21, 2014) [hereinafter "ICCPR Concluding Observations"], ¶ 5.

18 Israel-PLO Declaration of Principles, supra n. 11, art. V(3).

over Palestinians in East Jerusalem. The only power exercising authority in oEJ is Israel: it maintains effective jurisdiction over the territory and thus is bound by international human rights law.

3. Peremptory Norms (Jus Cogens)[19]

Peremptory norms are the prevailing norms of customary international law upon which the international system is premised. They are accepted and recognized as absolutely binding by the international community, and no derogation from these norms is permitted. While there is no authoritative list of jus cogens norms, the following principles relevant to this submission are generally recognized as jus cogens:

- The obligation to respect the right of self-determination,[20] and the corresponding prohibitions on the acquisition of territory, and the establishment and maintenance of colonial domination, by force.[21]

- The prohibition on institutionalized and systematic racial segregation and apartheid.[22]

F. Israeli Policy in occupied East Jerusalem

Israel's overarching policy in East Jerusalem is to establish facts on the ground that perpetuates and solidifies continued Jewish-Israeli domination of the city and the surrounding areas. Israeli policies and practices in oEJ—including those witnessed this summer—are designed and implemented

---

19 See generally Al-Haq Organization, "State Responsibility in Connection with Israel's Illegal Settlement Enterprise in the Occupied Palestinian Territory" (July 16, 2012), http://www.alhaq.org/images/stories/PDF/2012/Legal_Memo_State_Responsibility_FINAL_16_07.pdf.

20 International Law Commission, Draft Articles on Responsibility of States for Internationally Wrongful Acts, with commentaries, in Report of the International Law Commission, 53rd Session, UN Doc. No. A/56/10 (2001), ¶¶ 76 et seq. [hereinafter "ILC Draft Articles on State Responsibility"], commentary, Art. 40, ¶ 5, available at http://legal.un.org/ilc/texts/instruments/english/commentaries/9_6_2001.pdf.

21 FN 651.

22 FN 651, Commentary Art. 40, ¶ 4.

in order to facilitate this by: 1) changing the demographic make-up of the city by forcibly displacing Palestinians from East Jerusalem; and 2) severing East Jerusalem from the remainder of the West Bank.

1. Changing the Demographic Makeup of the City

In 1973, the Israeli government adopted the recommendation of the inter-ministerial Gafni Committee that the maintenance of the then-existing "demographic balance" of municipal Jerusalem – 27% Palestinian and 73% Israeli – should be a state policy objective. Since the Gafni Committee, all municipal forecasts addressed the issue of this perceived demographic 'threat,' and became the starting point of every development plan for Israeli-defined municipal Jerusalem.[23]

For various reasons, Israel has been unable to achieve its demographic objectives. Fewer settlers have moved to East Jerusalem than Israeli leaders had hoped, while higher Palestinian birth rates relative to Jewish Israelis has increased the percentage of Palestinians living in the city. The most recent Jerusalem Master Plan revised the demographic target to a more 'modest' 60 percent Jewish, 40 percent Arab. Nevertheless, the Master Plan emphasizes the importance of maintaining a Jewish majority in the city, and how the municipality's plans support this.

Israel's "demographic balance" policy has two primary aspects. First, it seeks to decrease the Palestinian population of East Jerusalem through a pervasive set of governmental policies resulting in forced displacement. This includes forbidding new Palestinian construction in Palestinian areas and a draconian residency system that strips Palestinians of their residency rights in Jerusalem. While Palestinians in East Jerusalem are subject to Israeli civil law—theoretically, the same as Israeli Jews—there is systematic, institutionalized and pervasive discrimination against Palestinians in its application and enforcement by ISF. The Israeli policies of forced transfer of Palestinians in East Jerusalem are widely known. It is commonly understood by the local population that the municipality wants to make the lives of Palestinians so miserable that they simply leave

---

23 See B'Tselem, "A Policy of Discrimination: Land Expropriation, Planning and Building in East Jerusalem" (1995) at 31,http://www.btselem.org/publications/summaries/199505_policy_of_discrimination (discussing Gafni Commission); Nadav Shragai, "Demography, Geopolitics, and the Future of Israel's Capital: Jerusalem's Proposed Master Plan" (Jerusalem Center for Public Affairs, 2010) at 11, http://jcpa.org/wp-content/uploads/2012/04/Jerusalem-Master-Plan.pdf (discussing Jerusalem 2020 Master Plan).

Jerusalem.[24]

The second objective of Israel's policy of demographic balance is to increase the population of illegal Jewish-Israeli settlers in East Jerusalem.

a. Forced Transfer of the Palestinian Population of East Jerusalem

i. Israeli law in occupied East Jerusalem

As a result of the unlawful annexation, Palestinians in East Jerusalem are governed by domestic Israeli law and not subject to the Israeli military regime governing Palestinians elsewhere in the OPT. Even within its domestic legal framework, however, forced transfer of Palestinians is institutionalized. Israel maintains a three-tiered system which accords different civil status, rights and legal protections for Jewish Israeli citizens, Palestinian citizens of Israel and Palestinian residents of East Jerusalem.[25] The skeleton of this three-tiered system is legislation, including many quasi-constitutional Basic Laws, which:

- Define Israel (including occupied East Jerusalem) as the "state of the Jewish people" (e.g., Basic Law: the Knesset (1958) and Amendment 9 (1985); Basic Law: Human Dignity and Liberty (1992));

- Grant "Jewish nationality" and Israeli citizenship to the Jewish population, including immigrants, i.e., the status of nationals with full civil and political rights to and in the country (e.g., Law of Return (1950); Citizenship Law (1952));[26]

---

24 For a more comprehensive overview of Israeli policies of forcible transfer in East Jerusalem, see Civic Coalition for Defending Palestinians' Rights in Jerusalem, "Aggressive Urbanism: Urban Planning and the Displacement of Palestinians within and from Occupied East Jerusalem" (Dec. 2009), http://civiccoalition-jerusalem.org/system/files/documents/aggressive_urbanism.pdf.

25 This system is four-tiered if Palestinian refugees of 1948 and 1967 are considered. The refugees, who were not present during respective Israeli population censuses, were excluded from entitlement to Israeli citizenship or Jerusalem residency.

- Convey the status of Israeli citizens without a nationality to the descendants of Palestinians recorded in the first Israeli population census in 1952, i.e., an inferior civil status that does not recognize their indigenous status in the country and conveys limited civil and political rights (Citizenship Law (1952));

- Assign the status of "permanent residents" of Jerusalem to Palestinians recorded in the first Israeli population census in occupied East Jerusalem in 1967, i.e., the status accorded to non-Jewish long-term residents that does not convey the rights of citizens, including no protected right to stay, leave and return to their country (Entry into Israel Law (1952); Entry into Israel Regulations (1974));

- Authorize/regulate irreversible confiscation of Palestinian property and resources and permanent transfer of ownership to the state and the Jewish National Fund (JNF) (e.g., Absentees' Property Law (1950); Development Authority (Transfer of Property) Law (1950); Land Acquisition for Public Purposes Ordinance (1943); Basic Law: Israel Lands (1960));

- Allow claims of pre-1948 Jewish property in East Jerusalem but no Palestinian claims of pre-1948 property in West Jerusalem (Legal and Administrative Matters (Regulation) Law (Consolidated Version) (1970));

- Grant public status and functions to private Zionist organizations, such as the Jewish Agency, World Zionist Organization and Jewish National Fund, which are mandated to develop confiscated Palestinian land for settlement exclusively by Jews (World Zionist Organization-Jewish Agency Status Law

---

26 As observed by Miloon Kothari, former UN Special Rapporteur on adequate housing, the official Israeli translation of the Ezrahut (Hebrew for citizenship) Law (1952) as "Nationality Law" is misleading, because Israeli law does not recognize an Israeli nationality, instead recognizing the distinct concepts of Israeli citizenship and Jewish nationality. See Report of the Special Rapporteur on adequate housing as a component of the right to an adequate standard of living, Miloon Kothari, UN Commission on Human Rights, Fifty-ninth session (15 June 2002) at 23 n. 4. See also HCJ 630/70 Tamarin v. State of Israel, 26(1) P.D. 197, 205 (1972) (affirming absence of Israeli nationality) ("There is no Israeli nation separate from the Jewish People. The Jewish People is composed not only of those residing in Israel but also of Diaspora Jewry.")

(1952); Jewish National Fund Law (1953); Covenant with Zionist Executive (1954)).[27]

For Palestinians, the combination of these laws has resulted in a system that fails to protect the rights to freedom of movement and residency, land and property in occupied East Jerusalem. The system legitimizes and facilitates expropriation and forcible displacement of Palestinians while providing strong legal protections to Israel's privileged Jewish population.

ii. Permanent Residency for the Indigenous Population

When Israel annexed East Jerusalem in 1967, the Palestinians within Israeli-defined borders were not granted Israeli citizenship, but rather residency permits, commonly known as "Jerusalem IDs." The Jerusalem IDs are the equivalent of a permanent residency status. Palestinians are required to continuously establish that their "center of life" is in Israel, including Israeli-defined municipal Jerusalem.

Palestinians that fail to prove that their "center of life" is in Jerusalem are at a constant risk of having their permanent residency status revoked, and would lose their ability to continue living in East Jerusalem. In order to push Palestinians to live outside of the Jerusalem municipal boundaries, Israel has engaged in an elaborate set of policies to limit physical Palestinian growth and ability to live a normal and dignified life. This has driven Palestinians to parts of municipal Jerusalem that are "outside the wall," where Israel permits unlicensed construction while providing virtually no municipal services.[28] Others are forced to move outside the municipal boundaries altogether, and thus place themselves at great risk of losing their Jerusalem ID if discovered.[29]

---

27 For an overview of discriminatory Israeli laws, see Adalah: The Legal Center for Arab Minority Rights in Israel, "Discriminatory Laws Database," http://adalah.org/eng/Israeli-Discriminatory-Law-Database.

28 It is widely believed that Israel intends to adopt the route of its wall as Jerusalem's new municipal borders and revoke the Jerusalem residency rights of Palestinians living in Jerusalem neighborhoods east of the wall. See Al-Haq Organization, "The Jerusalem Trap: The Looming Threat Posed by Israel's Annexationist Policies in Occupied East Jerusalem" (2010), http://www.alhaq.org/publications/publications-index/item/the-jerusalem-trap. Such measures would validate the ICJ's concern in its 2004 advisory opinion that the wall "could well become permanent" and "would be tantamount to de facto annexation." Consequences of a Wall, supra n. 2, ¶ 121.

iii. Restrictive Zoning/Inability to Build

Racially-restrictive urban planning and zoning is central to Israeli efforts to forcibly displace the Palestinian population in Jerusalem. Of the area annexed from the West Bank in 1967 and redrawn into the Israeli municipal borders of East Jerusalem, only 13 percent is zoned for Palestinian construction, and most of this area is already densely built-up. Most of the remaining land area has been confiscated and allocated to existing and planned Israeli settlements and the network of roads connecting them and tying them into West Jerusalem and Israel.

b. Increasing the Population of Illegal Jewish-Israeli Settlers

The UN-created 2013 International Fact-Finding Mission on Israeli Settlements concluded that the Israeli government plays a "leading role" in settlement construction and expansion.[30] The Fact-Finding Mission further concluded that:

> Since 1967, the State of Israel has directly participated in the planning of settlements through provisions in its planning policies... Israel has also supported settlements in the [oPt] through other mean, including by legalizing outposts, controlling land in which settlements are subsequently built, providing them with infrastructure and public services, granting benefits and incentives to settlers and sponsoring economic activities."[31]

The Israeli government makes a concerted effort to increase the population of illegal Israeli settlers in a variety of ways.

---

29 It has been widely understood that Israel is using the wall as a political barrier in this regard. Israeli leaders, including Mayor Nir Barakat, have openly spoken about redrawing the municipal boundaries to follow the wall. See Melanie Lidman, "Barakat proposes changing Jerusalem's borders," Jerusalem Post (Dec. 17, 2011), available at http://www.jpost.com/National-News/Barkat-proposes-changing-Jerusalems-borders.

30 Report of the independent international fact-finding mission to investigate the implications of the Israeli settlements on the civil, political, economic, social and cultural rights of the Palestinian people throughout the Occupied Palestinian Territory, including East Jerusalem, UN Doc. No. A/HRC/22/63 (Feb. 7, 2013) [hereinafter "Settlements FFM Report"], § IV.

31 Settlements FFM Report, supra n. 31, at ¶ 15.

First, Israel expropriates lands in East Jerusalem for the construction of Jewish-only settlements and 'green spaces' such as nature reserves and public parks. These green spaces, such as the proposed Mt. Scopus Slopes Park, are purposefully built to prevent the growth of Palestinian neighborhoods.[32] The government's reliance on Israeli law to justify these expropriations are irrelevant: as the occupying power in East Jerusalem, Israel is bound by international humanitarian law and may only expropriate land when absolutely necessary for legitimate military needs.

Moreover, the government issues tenders and authorizes the construction of several thousand new housing units in occupied East Jerusalem every year. These units and settlements come are serviced by public services and infrastructure of modern cities, including a road network that connects East Jerusalem settlements with population centers in Israel as well as other settlements in the West Bank.

Such actions by the Israeli government produce the allure of normalcy, as if the settlements are just another part of Israel—connected to its public transport system, its electricity grid, its water system, and all the other amenities that Israelis living within pre-1967 borders of Israel may enjoy.

Second, the Israeli government incentivizes Jewish Israelis to move to East Jerusalem settlements. Israel incentivizes settlement in East Jerusalem through its extensive connection and seamless integration to West Jerusalem and Israel, including a light-rail line connecting the East Jerusalem settlements to West Jerusalem. Moreover, as housing prices in West Jerusalem rise, many of the East Jerusalem settlements, such as Pisgat Zeev and Neve Yakouv, are working-class and provide an affordable alternative for lower-income Jewish Israelis.

4. Severing East Jerusalem from the Remainder of the West Bank

Since the peace negotiations began in 1993, Israel has consolidated its hold on four large "blocs" of settlements surrounding the municipal

32 See, e.g., Nir Hasson, "Israel fast tracks construction of national park between two Palestinian villages," Haaretz (Nov. 14, 2013), http://www.haaretz.com/news/diplomacy-defense/1.558090 (observing that "an employee of the Israel Nature and Parks Authority was recorded admitting that the purpose of establishing the Mount Scopus park at a site between the [Jerusalem] villages of Isawiyah and A-Tur is to block Palestinian development there, rather than to preserve nature.")

boundaries of Jerusalem, which house approximately 152,000 Israeli settlers.[33] These include the settlement "blocs" south of Jerusalem for which Israel has recently expropriated thousands of dunums near the Palestinian village of Wadi Fukin, which represents Israel's single largest expropriation of Palestinian land in three decades. Throughout the peace process, Israel has consistently built within these settlement "blocs," arguing that they will remain under Israeli control under any final-status agreement.

These settlement blocs sever occupied East Jerusalem from the rest of the West Bank. Currently, the settlements completely surround the vast majority of Palestinian areas in East Jerusalem, threatening the link between East Jerusalem and the rest of the West Bank, and thus the viability of a Palestinian state. If Israel proceeds with its planned expansion of the Ma'ale Adumim settlement into the "E1" area, it will sever the last link between occupied East Jerusalem, and the rest of the West Bank.

Moreover, the settlement blocs prevent the natural expansion of Palestinian neighborhoods within municipal Jerusalem, and Palestinian cities in the West Bank that would otherwise grow to form a Palestinian Jerusalem metropolitan area, stretching from Ramallah in the north to Bethlehem in the south. Without space for natural growth and expansion, infrastructure and resources are pushed beyond capacity.

In addition to dissecting the Palestinian areas of the West Bank, the settlement blocs distort the demographic balance of Greater Jerusalem. If and when Israel formally annexes these settlement blocs to municipal Jerusalem, the Palestinian presence in Jerusalem will be further marginalized and the Palestinians' ability to challenge their dispossession from Jerusalem further reduced.

---

33 These settlements and settlement blocs include the Adumim Bloc, Etzion Bloc, and Givat Ze'ev.

II. Israeli Violence Against Palestinians and State Attribution

A. Introduction

Israel's effective annexation of East Jerusalem in June 1967 facilitated the illegal transfer of Israeli nationals into East Jerusalem. Since 1967, all of Israel's governments have supported the settlement enterprise, which violates the prohibition against transferring, directly or indirectly, the Occupying Power's civilian population into the occupied territory. Specifically, the settlement enterprise violates Geneva Convention (IV) Article 49(6) and customary international humanitarian law.[34] It is a grave breach under Additional Protocol I to the Geneva Conventions and a war crime under the Rome Statute of the International Criminal Court.[35] Insofar as the settlement enterprise displaces Palestinians through land expropriations, closed military zones, and settler violence, it also violates the prohibition on forced population transfer.[36] This has been affirmed by decades of international consensus and by the International Court of Justice in its 2004 Legal Consequences of a Wall Advisory Opinion.

The International Fact-Finding Mission on Israeli Settlements in the Occupied Palestinian Territory, in its February 2013 report, found that settler violence and intimidation dates back to at least 1973 and aims to pressure Palestinians to leave their lands.[37] As Israel has expanded its settlement enterprise, violence by settlers and non-settler Israeli civilians

---

34 Legal Consequences of a Wall, supra n. 2, at ¶ 120; see also International Committee of the Red Cross, Customary International Humanitarian Law, Volume I: Rules (Jean-Marie Henckaerts and Louise Doswald-Beck, eds., 2005), available at https://www.icrc.org/customary-ihl/eng/docs/v1 [hereinafter "ICRC Customary IHL Rules"], "Rule 130: States may not deport or transfer parts of their own civilian population into a territory they occupy" (collecting authorities).

35 Israel is not a party to Additional Protocol I or to the Rome Statute of the International Criminal Court.

36 For example, Israel's "E1" plan aims to connect the Adumim Bloc settlements to East Jerusalem. To achieve this goal, Israel is forcibly transferring Bedouin communities to the Jericho area in violation of its obligations under Geneva Convention (IV) and customary international humanitarian law. See United Nations Office for the Coordination of Humanitarian Affairs, occupied Palestinian territory [hereinafter "UN OCHA oPt"], "Bedouin Communities at Risk of Forcible Transfer," Sept. 2014, https://www.ochaopt.org/documents/ocha_opt_communities_jerusalem_factsheet_september_2014_english.pdf.

37 Settlements FFM Report, supra n. 31, at ¶ 51.

against Palestinians has increased. The systematic lack of due diligence by the Israeli authorities in preventing and investigating private violence against civilians is illustrative of Israel's culture of impunity for human rights violations against Palestinians. In extreme instances, Israeli officials have condoned—and even called for—the commission of violence against Palestinians. Settler violence against Palestinians surged during the military operations conducted since 13 June 2014, particularly after the bodies of the three teenage settlers were found in the West Bank on June 30.

International law recognizes state responsibility for private conduct by non-state actors under certain conditions. This submission contends that Israel is responsible for acts of private violence against Palestinian by Israeli civilians, including settlers. It argues that violence by Israeli civilians against Palestinians is attributable to the State of Israel on two bases:

1. Impunity: Israel's systematic failure to protect the Palestinian population in the oPt and to provide an effective remedy for violations; and

2. Incitement: Israeli state actors have accepted, approved of, and even encouraged violence by Israelis against Palestinians. This culture of impunity, coupled with dehumanizing representations of Palestinians by Israeli public officials, establish that Israel has acknowledged and adopted settler violence as state conduct.

Section B of this section outlines the legal framework of state responsibility for private acts. Section C attributes private violence against Palestinians by Israeli civilians, including settlers, to the State of Israel under the theories of impunity and incitement. Section D details acts of settler violence against Palestinians in occupied East Jerusalem.

B. Legal Framework for State Responsibility for Private Violence

It is accepted customary international law and customary international humanitarian law that States are responsible for their internationally-wrongful acts.[38] States are responsible both for breaches committed by state organs and breaches committed by non-state entities that are attributable to the state under international law.[39] Conduct attributable to the state may consist of acts, omissions, or a combination of acts and omissions.[40]

Article 11 of the ILC Draft Articles on State Responsibility provides that private conduct will be considered an act of State under international law "if and to the extent that the State acknowledges and adopts the conduct in question as its own."[41] The state's acknowledgment and adoption of the private conduct must be clear and can be retroactive.[42] Acknowledgment and adoption of conduct must be more than mere support, approval, or endorsement and can take the form of either words or conduct.[43] It is also possible for the state to adopt conduct without necessarily approving of it.[44] Finally, acknowledgement and adoption of conduct by the state can be express or it can be inferred from the State's conduct.[45]

Customary international humanitarian law likewise recognizes that "[s]tate responsibility for acts committed by private individuals or groups can arise through subsequent acknowledgement and adoption of the acts of these persons or groups."[46] If the State acknowledges and adopts the conduct, that conduct becomes an acts of the State, regardless of whether the private actor was a State organ or was mandated to act on behalf of the State at the time of commission.[47]

Case law at the international and regional level further illuminates instances

---

38 ILC Draft Articles on State Responsibility, supra n. 20, art. 11.

39 Id., art. 2.

40 Id., art. 2, Commentary ¶ 4.

41 Id., art. 11.

42 Id., art. 11, Commentary ¶ 4.

43 Id., art. 11, Commentary ¶¶ 6, 8.

44 See Christine Chinkin, A Critique of the Public/Private Dimension, 10 Eur. J. Int'l L. 388 (1999), available at http://www.ejil.org/pdfs/10/2/588.pdf.

45 ILC Draft Articles on State Responsibility, supra n. 20, art. 11, Commentary ¶ 9.

46 ICRC Customary IHL Rules, supra n. 34, "Rule 149: A State is responsible for violations of international humanitarian law attributable to it, including … (d) violations committed by private persons or groups which it acknowledges and adopts as its own conduct."

47 Id.

in which the state is responsible for acts by private, non-state actors. The ICJ United States Diplomatic and Consular Staff in Tehran case illustrates an instance of ex post facto adoption by the state of internationally-wrongful conduct. The ICJ held Iran liable for the 1979 occupation of the United States Embassy in Tehran and the hostage-taking of embassy staff by private Iranian nationals through its endorsement and maintenance of the internationally-wrongful situation:

> The policy thus announced by the Ayatollah Khomeini, of maintaining the occupation of the Embassy and the detention of its inmates as hostages for the purpose of exerting pressure on the United States Government was complied with by other Iranian authorities and endorsed by them repeatedly in statements made in various contexts. ... The approval given to these facts by the Ayatollah Khomeini and other organs of the Iranian State, and the decision to perpetuate them, translated continuing occupation of the Embassy and detention of the hostages into acts of that State.[48]

Iran's failure to take sufficient action to prevent or end the seizure was also noted by the ICJ. The ICJ described the repeated failure of the Iranian government to take any appropriate steps to protect the United States consulate staff and premises as rising to a level beyond 'mere negligence.'[49] While 'mere negligence' by the state does not attach responsibility, the ICJ indicated that in instances of awareness or conscious negligence by the state, the conduct is attributable to the state.[50]

The ICTY Appeals Chamber held in the Tadić (1999) that the state was responsible for the acts of individuals and groups that could be regarded as de facto agents if the act was publicly endorsed of approved ex post facto by the state.[51]

The principle that state responsibility attaches when the state fails to exercise due diligence in preventing and investigating abuses has been

---

48 United States Diplomatic and Consular Staff in Tehran (United States of America v. Iran), [1980] ICJ Rep. 3 (May 24, 1980), ¶ 74.

49 Id., ¶ 64

50 See Giuliana Ziccardi Capaldo, The Pillars of Global Law (2013) 261–62.

51 ICRC Customary IHL Rules, Rule 149, citing Prosecutor v. Furundžija, Case No. IT-95-17/1-T, Judgment (Dec. 10, 1998) ¶ 62 and Prosecutor v. Tadić, Case No. IT-94-1-A, Judgment on Appeal (July 15, 1999), ¶ 63.

held by regional human rights courts, as well. In Velasquez Rodriguez v. Honduras the Inter-American Court of Human Rights famously held that the state must exercise due diligence to prevent and respond to human rights violations—widespread disappearances and torture—committed by non-state actors which are not attributable to the state.[52]

State responsibility also attaches where private conduct is subsequently adopted by the state, as occurred with the capture of Adolf Eichmann by Israeli nationals in Buenos Aires in May 1960. Although Israel neither admitted nor denied Argentina's charge that it was involved in Eichmann's capture[53], its exercise of jurisdiction over Eichmann after his captors brought him to Israel was deemed to constitute adoption of the capture.[54]

C. Attribution of Private Acts of Violence to the State of Israel

1. Impunity

Israeli authorities have systematically failed to investigate and prosecute private violence by Israeli civilians, including settlers, against Palestinians, even though frequently the identity of perpetrators is known or can be easily determined; Israeli Security Forces are present at the scene; and witnesses and evidence are plentiful. In the rare instances investigations occur, they are ineffective and often close without indictments,[55] allowing impunity to prevail.[56] In fact, from 2006–2012, over 90% of complaints by

---

52 Osman v United Kingdom [1998] EHRR 101; see Chinkin, A Critique of the Public/Private Dimension, supra n. 44, at 394.

53 UNSC Res. 138 (1960) implied that the Israeli government was at least aware of, and consented to, the plan to capture Eichmann in Argentina, and thereby violated Argentina's sovereignty. This resolution is understood to endorse the 'acknowledgement and adoption' standard of attribution. See Capaldo, supra n. 50, at 261.

54 ILC Draft Articles on State Responsibility, supra n. 20, art. 11, Commentary ¶ 5.

55 Israeli investigations into complaints by Palestinians have been characterized by professional negligence, (e.g. lack of training, shortage of Arabic speakers), a lack of investigative action, and a failure to meet acceptable investigation standards. See generally Yesh Din, "Semblance of Law: Law Enforcement Upon Israeli Civilians in the West Bank," (Sept. 11, 2006), available at http://www.yesh-din.org/userfiles/file/Reports-English/SemblanceofLawfullreportEng.pdf.

56 Settlements FFM Report, supra n. 31, at ¶ 107.

Palestinians about private violence were closed without indictments, but only 5-10% of complaints by Israelis against Palestinians do not reach the court.[57] The lack of due diligence exercised by the state in preventing and investigating private violence against Palestinians imputes responsibility to Israel for such acts.

Israeli authorities have not attempted to protect Palestinians from attacks by Israelis, in violation of Israel's obligations under the Geneva Conventions and IHRL. In documented instances, the Israeli Security Forces have been complicit in acts of violence against Palestinians either by participating in violence or witnessing but doing nothing to stop it. Israel's systematic failure to investigate and prosecute incidents of violence against Palestinians has led to a culture of impunity in which Israelis can attack Palestinians with no fear of repercussions.

The Israeli authorities' failure to effectively investigate and prosecute incidents of private violence violates of Israel's obligation to provide a right to a remedy under the ICCPR Article 2(3), CRC Article 39, and ICERD Article 6 as well as Hague Convention (IV) Article 3.[58] The rampant impunity for attacks by Israeli nationals against Palestinians—contrasted with the accountability for Palestinian attacks against Israelis—illustrates Israel's institutionalized discrimination against Palestinians. The difference in the legislative and administrative regime applied to Israelis and Palestinians violates the principle of non-discrimination, codified in ICCPR Article 2(1), and equal protection of the law, codified in ICCPR Article 26.[59]

The systematic lack of due diligence by Israeli authorities and impunity for private violence is tantamount to Israel acknowledging and adopting private violence as its own conduct.[60]
If Israel did not acknowledge and adopt this conduct as its own, it would

57 The Israeli NGO Yesh Din found that of 880 investigations that were closed, 592 were closed due to the ISF's failure to identify and locate suspects, while 192 were closed due to insufficient evidence. See Yesh Din, Shadow Report to the Fourth Periodic Review of Israel [ICCPR], (Sept. 8, 2014), http://tbinternet.ohchr.org/Treaties/CCPR/Shared%20Documents/ISR/INT_CCPR_CSS_ISR_18231_E.pdf

58 UNGA Res. 60/147, Basic Principles and Guidelines on the Right to a Remedy and Reparation for Victims of Gross Violations of International Human Rights Law and Serious Violations of International Humanitarian Law, UN Doc. No. A /RES/60/147 (Dec. 16, 2005), available at http://www.ohchr.org/EN/ProfessionalInterest/Pages/RemedyAndReparation.aspx.

59 The Human Rights Committee most recently expressed concern about Israel's violations of the principles of non-discrimination and equality in its concluding observations on the fourth periodic report of Israel, issued October 28, 2014. See ICCPR Concluding Observations, supra n. 17, at ¶ 7.

have made serious efforts to protect Palestinians and to provide an effective remedy, including effective investigations, for acts of private violence against Palestinians. Israel's sustained failure to protect Palestinians in Jerusalem, considered in light of its policy objective of maintaining a sizeable Jewish-Israeli majority in the city, leads to the conclusion that it has adopted private violence by Israelis against Palestinians as part of its policies and practices of demographic dominance. Under the ICJ's analysis in the United States Diplomatic and Consular Staff in Tehran case, Israel is responsible for private violence because of its awareness of, and repeated failure to address, these abuses.

Moreover, Israelis attack Palestinians to force them to leave their homes and lands[61], in alignment with Israel's policies that forcibly transfer Palestinians out of the oPt and transfer settlers, into the oPt, in violation of international humanitarian law.[62] Israel's refusal to prevent private violence and intimidation towards Palestinians is an integral part of its plans to populate the oPt with Israeli settlers. Thus, the culture of impunity is a consequence of Israel's plans to force the occupied Palestinian population out of the oPt and transfer its Israeli population into the territories. The intentional nature of Israel's inaction with respect to securing justice for Palestinians is yet another indicator that the state has adopted the conduct of private violence.

Finally, although this submission focuses on settler violence in occupied East Jerusalem, it should be noted that incidents of racist mobs of settler and non-settler Israelis committing and inciting violence against Palestinians in West Jerusalem and other parts of Israel have also contributed to the culture of impunity.[63] In addition to the attacks in

---

60 The state's acknowledgment and adoption of the private conduct must be clear and must be more than mere support, approval, or endorsement and can take the form of either words or conduct. It can also be retroactive. ILC Draft Articles on State Responsibility, supra n. 20, art. 11, Commentary ¶ 4, 6, 8.

61 Settlements FFM Report, supra n. 31, ¶ 50; see also United Nations Office of the High Commissioner for Human Rights, "Update on Settler Violence in the West Bank, including East Jerusalem" (Oct. 2013) 4-5, http://unispal.un.org/pdfs/UHCHR_SettlerViolence.pdf; Israeli Committee Against House Demolitions, "Israel's Policy of Demolishing Palestinian Homes Must End: A Submission to the UN Human Rights Council" (Mar. 2012), http://www.icahd.org/node/458 (discussing the displacement of several hundred Palestinians following incidents of settler violence, evictions, and military training).

62 Geneva Convention (IV), art. 49.

occupied East Jerusalem delineated later in this submission, several attacks occurred in West Jerusalem over the summer, particularly along Jaffa Street.[64] Settlers violently mobbed trains and workplaces to beat Palestinians and also attacked Palestinians on the street and Palestinian taxi drivers.[65] Although these acts, which were committed outside the oPt, do not constitute settler violence per se, they indicate the widespread culture of impunity that pervades all parts of Israel and the oPt.

5. Incitement

Israeli officials have also incited Israelis to commit human rights violations against Palestinians. This section will first outline the legal framework for incitement under international criminal law and international human rights law. Then it will provide examples of racist and hateful rhetoric employed by officials before analyzing how such speech was tantamount to incitement.

a. Incitement to Genocide Under International Criminal Law

Direct and public incitement to genocide is prohibited under the Genocide Convention.[66] Thus, incitement to genocide includes incitement to commit any of the following acts with the intent to destroy, in whole or in part, a

---

63 In Haifa, an Israeli mob shouting "Death to Arabs" brutally beat the Palestinian deputy mayor and his son in response to a rally against Israel's onslaught in Gaza. After 200 children died from Israel's bombs, mobs in Tel Aviv chanted "Tomorrow there's no school in Gaza, they don't have any children left" (which rhymes in Hebrew). The ISF stood by and allowed racist Israeli mobs to commit and incite violence against Palestinians with impunity. See "Tomorrow there's no school in Gaza, they don't have any children left – Israeli chant," Mondoweiss (July 28, 2014), http://mondoweiss.net/2014/07/tomorrow-children-israeli.

64 Rania Khalek, "Merciless Israeli mobs are hunting Palestinians," Electronic Intifada, July 27, 2014, http://electronicintifada.net/blogs/rania-khalek/merciless-israeli-mobs-are-hunting-palestinians.

65 See, e.g., Palestinian Centre for Human Rights, "Weekly Report On Israeli Human Rights Violations in the Occupied Palestinian Territory (26 June – 02 July 2014)," (July 3, 2014) http://www.pchrgaza.org/portal/en/index.php?option=com_content&view=article&id=10445:weekly-report-on-israeli-human-rights-violations-in-the-occupied-palestinian-territory-26-june--02-july-2014-&catid=84:weekly-2009&Itemid=183;

"Settlers assault Palestinian cab drivers in Jerusalem," World Bulletin (Nov. 11, 2014) http://www.worldbulletin.net/middle-east/148158/settlers-assault-palestinian-cab-drivers-in-jerusalem.

66 Convention on the Prevention and Punishment of the Crime of Genocide, 78 U.N.T.S. 277 (Dec. 9, 1948) [hereinafter "Genocide Convention"], art. 3(c).

national, ethnical, racial or religious group:

(a) Killing members of the group;
(b) Causing serious bodily or mental harm to members of the group;
(c) Deliberately inflicting on the group conditions of life calculated to bring about its physical destruction in whole or in part;
(d) Imposing measures intended to prevent births within the group;
(e) Forcibly transferring children of the group to another group.[67]

The perpetrator must possess (1) the intent to directly prompt or provoke another to commit genocide and (2) the specific intent to destroy, in whole or in part, a protected group.[68]

Incitement to genocide has been recognized as an international crime since the International Military Tribunal at Nuremberg. It is an inchoate offense: the genocide urged by the incitement does not have to materialize in order for criminal liability to attach.[69] The danger that follows incitement—aside from the commission of the crime—is the creation of an atmosphere or state of mind among a large group that facilitates further acts of incitement and the commission of the genocide itself.[70]

b. Incitement Under International Human Rights Law

Both the ICCPR Article 20(2) and ICERD Article 4(a) prohibit any expression tantamount to incitement to discrimination, hostility or violence. The CERD Committee has generally emphasized that hate speech can contribute to

---

67 Genocide Convention, art. 2

68 Prosecutor v. Akayesu, Case No. ICTR-96-4-T, Judgment (Sept. 2, 1998).

69 The Trial Chamber of the International Criminal Tribunal for Rwanda held in Akayesu that because genocide is so serious a crime, incitement to genocide must be punishable even if the result expected by the perpetrator does not occur. See Wibke Kristin Timmermann, Incitement in International Criminal Law, 88 Int'l R. Red Cross 825, 840-841 (2006), available at https://www.icrc.org/eng/assets/files/other/irrc_864_timmermann.pdf.

70 For example, an appeals court affirmed the guilt of Hans Fritzsche, a senior official in Goebbels' Ministry of Popular Enlightenment and Propaganda who headed its Radio Division from 1942, noting how he used propaganda to knowingly contribute to creating a "mood" among Germans that facilitated the persecution and annihilation of the Jewish people. More recently, in the ICTR's Media Case, the Tribunal characterized incitement as a continuous crime because it can have long-term effects on people's minds. Prosecutor v. Nahimana et al. ("Media Case"), Case No. ICTR-99-52-T, Judgment (Dec. 3, 2003). See Timmermann, supra n. 69, at 830, 842.

racial violence and even genocide.[71]

ICCPR Article 20(2) states:

> Any advocacy of national, racial or religious hatred that constitutes incitement to discrimination, hostility or violence shall be prohibited by law.

ICERD Article 4(a) mandates that States Parties:

> Shall declare an offence punishable by law all dissemination of ideas based on racial superiority or hatred, incitement to racial discrimination, as well as all acts of violence or incitement to such acts against any race or group of persons of another colour or ethnic origin, and also the provision of any assistance to racist activities, including the financing thereof.

ICERD Article 4(c) further mandates that States:

> Shall not permit public authorities or public institutions, national or local, to promote or incite racial discrimination.

As the prohibitions against incitement are more specific under the ICERD than the ICCPR, this submission analyzes incitement under the ICERD.

In August 2012, the CERD Committee elaborated the key factors for determining when racist hate speech is prohibited and tantamount to incitement. The Committee placed importance on:

(1) Severity: who made the statement,[72] what was the substantive content,[73] and the timing of the statement. The severity factor also takes into account how likely and imminent the harm was.[74]

---

71 Navi Pillay, "Freedom of Expression and incitement to hatred in the context of International Human Rights Law," Lecture at the London School of Economics (Feb. 15, 2013), available at http://www.ohchr.org/en/NewsEvents/Pages/DisplayNews.aspx?NewsID=13018&LangID=E.

72 Politicians and prominent members of political parties and public officials or persons of similar status are particularly able to incite human rights violations. Article 19, "Prohibiting incitement to discrimination, hostility or violence" (Dec. 2012) 30–31, http://www.article19.org/data/files/medialibrary/3548/ARTICLE-19-policy-on-prohibition-to-incitement.pdf.

73 The content can be evaluated by considering the level of advocacy involved in the speech, taking into account whether the audience faces serious danger from the targeted group, who was targeted, whether they were directly or indirectly named, whether dehumanizing speech was used, the tone or provocative nature of the speech, and whether the speech contain language that has a special or "loaded" meaning to the audience. Id. at 34-36.

The scope and extent of the expression is another indicator of severity.[75]

(2) Intent: notably, under CERD, there is no requirement to demonstrate intent to discriminate, as the mere spread of certain materials is prohibited.[76]

(3) Context: history of violence and persecution and institutionalized discrimination against the group targeted by the speech.[77]

(4) Causation: although inciting an act does not necessarily cause the act, courts often consider causation factors, such as the creation of an atmosphere more susceptible to ideas of discrimination, hostility, or violence.[78]

c. Incitement by Israeli State Actors

State actors have also supported, justified, and incited private violence by Israeli civilians. From 2012–2013, for instance, instances of incitement by Israeli elected representatives and public leaders nearly doubled from 60 to 107 cases.[79] The significant increase in incitement by state officials

---

74 To determine the likelihood of harm, courts have looked at whether the speech was understood by the audience as a call to commit acts of discrimination, hostility, or violence; whether the speaker influenced the audience; whether the audience had the means to commit acts of discrimination, hostility, or violence; and whether the targeted group had recently suffered discrimination, hostility, or violence. Id. at 39–40.

75 To determine the scope and extent of the incitement, courts have examined how accessible the message was to the public; whether it was directed at the general public; how was it disseminated; and the magnitude or intensity of the expression in terms of frequency, amount, and extent of communications. Id. at 37–39.

76 Under ICCPR Article 20(2), "advocacy" may be interpreted as requiring intent.

77 Article 19, "Prohibiting incitement to discrimination, hostility or violence," supra n. 72, at 29–30.

78 For example, in Ross v. Canada, the Supreme Court noted that the expression made by the petitioner, a teacher who published and made statements that were discriminatory towards Jews, may have contributed to a "poisoned environment" within the school district. Ross v. Canada, Communication No. 736/1997, U.N. Doc. CCPR/C/70/D/736/1997 (UN Human Rights Committee, 2000) at 54-64, available at http://www.ohchr.org/Documents/Publications/SDecisionsVol7en.pdf.

79 Coalition Against Racism in Israel, "Racism Report 2013," Main Findings (Mar. 21, 2013) http://www.fightracism.org/en/Article.asp?aid=398. The Report covers the period March 2012-February 2013. During this period, which includes "Operation Pillar of Defense," the November 2012 Israeli military operation in the Gaza Strip, acts of incitement by public officials specifically against Palestinians rose from 27 to 45. The 2014 Racism Report, covering March 2013-February 2014, during which time there were no major Israeli military operations, indicates a dramatic decrease in acts of incitement by Israel public officials. However, as shown herein, incitement by public officials and other public figures surged during the military operations conducted since 13 June 2014.

has also resulted in an increase in racially motivated incidents by Israelis against Palestinians. This incitement to violence perpetuates violence and impunity while also intimidating Palestinians into leaving their homes for fear of suffering greater violence. Moreover, private Israeli citizens also engaged in incitement against Palestinians, particularly through social media.[80]

The incitement by state actors to commit violence against Palestinians after the discovery of the three settlers' bodies permeates all levels of Israeli government, starting at the top with Prime Minister Benjamin Netanyahu. On June 30, Netanyahu sent a series of dehumanizing and provocative tweets, in which he referred to the Palestinian suspects in the killings as "human animals" and quoted "On the Slaughter" by Israel's national poet, Haim Bialik, about the 1903 Kishinev pogrom, in which dozens of Jews were murdered in present-day Moldova:

> With heavy grief we found 3 bodies. All signs indicate they are of our abducted youths Eyal, Gilad and Naftali. They were abducted & murdered in cold blood by human animals. ... Vengeance for the blood of a small child, Satan has not yet created. Neither has vengeance for the blood of 3 pure youths who were on their way home to their parents who will not see them anymore.

Netanyahu continued with this dehumanizing rhetoric in his July 1 eulogy for the three teenage settlers:

> The light you [the boy's families] radiate shines even brighter in contrast to the horrific darkness of those who seek our destruction—despicable kidnappers of children, heinous murderers whose brothers rejoice at the spilling of innocent blood. A deep and wide moral abyss separates us from our enemies. They sanctify death while we sanctify life. They sanctify cruelty while we sanctify compassion.

---

80 For instance, after the kidnapping of the three Israeli youth, the Facebook page "Until the boys are back, every hour we shoot a terrorist" was created, advocating for the murder of a Palestinian every hour until the youth were located. More than 16,000 persons joined this page, and many commenters to the page's thread called for kidnapping Palestinians in retaliation. Another Facebook page, "The People of Israel Demand Revenge," quickly gained more than 35,000 likes, mostly from young Israelis. Over 3,000 members joined another page, "If our boys are sitting in the dark, Palestinians will also sit in the dark," which called for Israel to cut off electricity to the West Bank and the Gaza Strip. Even before the kidnapping, Facebook pages such as the popular "We are all in favor of death to terrorists" page were replete with racial hatred and incitement to murder and torture Palestinians, including children.

Netanyahu's statements constitute incitement under the CERD Committee's standard. Netanyahu, who as head of state has immense authority, used provocative and dehumanizing rhetoric that promoted the idea that the "enemies"—the Palestinian people—are uncivilized, savage, and inherently violent. The timing of his remarks – during ongoing military operations and in the aftermath of the settlers' murders – made it likely that imminent harm would result. The context of his remarks – delivered to an angry Israeli population against the backdrop of the Israeli State's longstanding history of violence, persecution, and institutionalized discrimination against Palestinians – made this rhetoric particularly incendiary. By invoking the memory of pogroms against Jews in Europe, Netanyahu cynically promoted the idea that the murder of three teenagers reflected an existential threat to Israel's Jewish population and justified the disproportionate nature of the ongoing military operations. Netanyahu thereby drove the narrative that Palestinian acts of violence against Israelis are motivated not by Israel's denial of Palestinian self-determination, but by anti-Semitism and religious fundamentalism.

The Prime Minister's rhetoric encouraged other Israeli officials to incite violence against Palestinians. Ayelet Shaked, a Knesset member (MK) from the right-wing Jewish Home party, called for violence against Palestinian civilians on her Facebook wall by quoting a 2002 article by Eli Elitzur, then-editor of the conservative Israeli daily Makor Rishon. On July 1, Shaked posted this quote from Elitzur's article: "The reality is that this is a war between two people. Who is the enemy? The Palestinian people. Why? Ask them, they started it." The post garnered 1,000 shares and 4,000 "likes" within a week.[81]

The next day, a group of Israelis kidnapped and burned alive 16-year-old Mohammed Abu Khdeir. Even after this brutal murder, Shaked continued to post hate speech. On July 7, she posted another racist quote from Elitzur's article that advocated the murder of civilian Palestinian women:

> Behind every terrorist stand dozens of men and women, without whom he could not engage in terrorism. They are all enemy combatants, and their blood shall be on all their heads. Now this also includes the mothers of the martyrs, who send them to hell with flowers and kisses. They should follow their sons, nothing would be more just. They should go, as should the physical homes

---

81 Gideon Resnick, Israeli Politician Declares 'War' on 'the Palestinian People', The Daily Beast, July 7, 2014, Internet, http://www.thedailybeast.com/articles/2014/07/07/israeli-politician-declares-war-on-the-palestinian-people.html.

> in which they raised the snakes. Otherwise, more little snakes will be raised there.

Shaked's rhetoric, as the speech of an elected official, is attributable to the State as encouragement to commit violence against Palestinians.[82] The language of her July 7 post ("more little snakes") strongly implies an endorsement of violence, including the murder of Mohammed Abu Khdeir, which occurred between her posted quotes from Elitzur's article. Shaked used provocative and explicit dehumanizing language in calling Palestinians snakes and grossly generalizing all Palestinians as enemy combatants. Her words fanned the flames of racism, hate, and violence towards Palestinians.

Shaked's words also constitute incitement to genocide to the extent that her intent was to incite others to kill Palestinians; to deliberately destroy Palestinian homes in order to physically destroy the Palestinian people in whole or in part; and kill Palestinian mothers in order to prevent Palestinian births.

Israel has allowed racial hatred and discrimination—even incitement to commit grave human rights violations, including genocide—to spread in violation of its obligations under ICERD to condemn and eliminate racial discrimination.[83] Israel sanctions and facilitates this kind of speech because of its potential to intimidate Palestinians—who have no recourse for protection or justice—into leaving their land, thus freeing up space for the establishment of more settlements. When state actors incite acts of racial hatred and discrimination—including acts of racially motivated violence—it indicates that the state has also acknowledged and adopted such private conduct as its own.

6. Incidents of Israeli Violence Against Palestinians in occupied East Jerusalem

a. Murder: The Kidnapping and Death of Mohammed Abu Khdeir

The following incident of private violence violated Israel's obligation to

82 See Tadić, supra n. 51.

83 ICERD Article 2(d).

respect and protect the right to life (ICCPR Article 6; CRC Article 6); the prohibition against torture or cruel, inhuman or degrading treatment or punishment (ICCPR Article 7; CRC Article 37); and the right to liberty and security (ICCPR Article 9; CRC Article 37). It also violated the prohibition against the willful killing or inhuman treatment and against willfully causing great suffering or serious injury to body or health under customary international humanitarian law and Geneva Convention (IV) (Article 147). Finally, this incident violated Israel's obligation to respect and protect children affected by armed conflict.

On July 2, three Israelis—a settler from Adam settlement and his two 16-year-old accomplices—in a car kidnapped Mohammed Abu Khdeir (16 years old) and brutally tortured him before burning him alive. The 29-year-old ringleader behind the murder, Yosef Haim Ben-David, confessed that it was an act of revenge for the kidnapping and killing of the three teenage settlers. He told police in a statement that "'they took three of ours, let's take one of theirs,' and we decided to pick someone up, kidnap him, beat him within an inch of his life and discard of him." He wanted the victim "to know that he was about to die as a sacrifice for the Jews that were murdered."[84]

Mohammed was going to the mosque across the street from his family home in Shuafat when a car approached him and asked him directions to Tel Aviv. The Israelis forced Mohammed, who was kicking and screaming, into the vehicle, where he was brutally beaten. They subsequently drove to the Jerusalem Forest in West Jerusalem, where they forced Mohammed to drink gasoline and burned him alive.

The Abu Khdeir family learned about what happened to Mohammed from three Palestinian youths who had witnessed the kidnapping but were unable to stop it. When Mohammed's family reported the kidnapping, the Israeli Security Forces detained and questioned Mohammed's father for several hours while failing to review footage from surveillance cameras in the area. In fact, they damaged the film from the surveillance cameras and from a camera belonging to one of the Abu Khdeir's neighbors.

The Israeli Security Forces did not immediately respond when the Abu Khdeir family reported Mohammed was missing. Instead, they began spreading rumors that the family had murdered Mohammed in an honor

---

84 Daniel K. Eisenbud, Abu Khdeir murder suspect recounts grisly killing, The Jerusalem Post, Aug. 13, 2014, Internet, http://www.jpost.com/National-News/Abu-Khdeir-murder-suspect-recounts-grisly-killing-370911.

killing for being a homosexual. The Israeli Security Forces also sabotaged footage from surveillance cameras that identified Mohammed's attackers. They failed to properly investigate this footage, which could have saved Mohammed's life, and instead remained focused on investigating the family.

Mohammed's father gave the following account of the aftermath of Muhammad's kidnapping:

> We called the police. They didn't do anything. ... Instead of following the car which kidnapped him ... the police were in the area until 5 o'clock checking on the [surveillance] cameras. They didn't follow the car. Around 5 or 6 [in the morning] they took me to interrogation and kept me there until 11 [at night]. They were asking me: "Who are your enemies? What happened?" ... I told them "what are you talking about, what enemies? It's clear on the cameras that he was kidnapped." So the police asked me "how do you know they are Jewish?" I told them it's very clear, it's on the camera. ... They took the camera of our neighbors. They took the film ... they ruined the films and gave us back the films and they were not working, so that we could not make use of the evidence on the film. So all we have is what we managed to get from one camera [one that the authorities failed to confiscate]. The pictures were very clear and it was very clear, those who kidnapped my son. If it hadn't been for the camera, nobody would know what happened to my son. They could have found any other excuse.[85]

In addition to destroying evidence, Mohammed's father said the Israeli Security Forces were reluctant to run DNA tests and confirm that they found Mohammed's body. He described the lack of effective remedies for violations against Palestinians—especially in comparison with the timely, effective remedies for violations against Israelis.

> I was in the Maskobiyya [Russian Compound] detention center until 3 o'clock [on July 3rd]. Then they told us that they found a burned body, but they didn't know whose body it was. I asked them to show me a picture, and they refused. Then they told me they needed to take DNA samples from me and his mother to see if it was our son. ... At 11 p.m., they informed our lawyer that the burned body was that of my son. So the Israeli police tried to say

85 Interview with CCPRJ fieldworker, East Jerusalem, 29 October 2014. The interviewee asked to remain anonymous for reasons of personal security.

> it was a family problem, an internal problem between the family ... but because we have the film from the camera, they can't change the facts. After a few days, they declared that they caught those that committed the crime. But they said they weren't 100% sure. ... Eventually, those caught confessed that they committed the crime. But if they had wanted, they could have caught them within five minutes. In the street, there were at least 20 cameras for the light rail, which took pictures of everything happening. But the police told us these cameras were not working.[86]

The Israeli Security Forces wanted to perform an autopsy—which Mohammed's father did not want—as part of the investigation. Mohammed's father agreed to the autopsy as long as a Palestinian doctor was part of the autopsy team, which led to the involvement of Dr. Saeed al Alul from Al Quds University. Mohammed's father indicated that the presence of a Palestinian doctor allowed him to have faith in the autopsy process.

> In the autopsy report, [Dr. Saeed al Alul] said that they had burned Mohammed while he was still alive because they found smoke in his lungs. They gave us the report after two weeks. This is all due to the presence of the Palestinian doctor; otherwise they [the police] would have changed the facts, because they are very well known for changing facts and lying about us. They have laws, but the law only applies to us. Law is not applied to the Israelis or the Jewish settlers.[87]

According to Mohammed's father, the same group who murdered Mohammed attempted to kidnap 9-year-old Mousa Rami Zaloum from their neighborhood the day before they abducted Mohammed.

> The Israeli government is responsible. It is a right wing government. Two days before the death of my son, there was a demonstration for right wing settlers and they were calling "Death to Arabs" during the demonstration. The government didn't do anything, didn't stop them. Instead, they protected them. ... The day before [Mohammed's kidnapping] there was an attempted kidnapping, but the police did nothing. They were five people with the same car. They tried to kidnap the Zaloum family's son. The police did

---

86 Id.

87 Id.

nothing.[88]

The inaction by the authorities concerning the attempted kidnapping of Mousa is part of the larger culture of impunity under which Israelis are not deterred from perpetrating any number of abuses against Palestinians.

b. Physical Attacks

Each of the following incidents of private violence by Israeli civilians violated the prohibition against torture or cruel, inhuman or degrading treatment or punishment (ICCPR Article 7) and violated the prohibition against inhuman treatment and willfully causing great suffering or serious injury to body or health under customary international humanitarian law and Geneva Convention (IV) (Article 147).

Israel is responsible for the following incidents because the impunity with which the perpetrator (s) committed violence against Palestinian(s) indicates that Israel acknowledged and adopted the private conduct as its own.

- On July 3, an Israeli shot Ali Ahmed Abu Samra (30 years old) in the leg near Al-Ram, northern East Jerusalem. The perpetrator managed to escape in his vehicle.[89]
- On July 5, a group of Israelis accompanied by the Israeli Security Forces raided Sheikh Jarrah neighborhood and smashed the windows of at least seven cars. When the Palestinian residents tried to throw the settlers out, the Israeli Security Forces fired tear gas and used sticks to attack the Palestinians. As a result of this assault, five boys and one girl sustained wounds and minor bruises. The Israeli Security Forces arrested three Palestinians following this incident: Ahmed al-Sabbagh (24 years old), Mahmoud al-Sabbagh (19 years old), and Muahmmed al-Shawish (20 years old).[90]
    - The arrest of the Palestinians and blatant disregard for

---

88 Id.

89 Weekly Report On Israeli Human Rights Violations in the Occupied Palestinian Territory (03 – 09 July 2014), Palestinian Centre for Human Rights (PCHR), July 10, 2014, Internet, http://www.pchrgaza.org/portal/en/index.php?option=com_content&view=article&id=10489:weekly-report-on-israeli-human-rights-violations-in-the-occupied-palestinian-territory-03-09-july-2014&catid=84:weekly-2009&Itemid=183.

90 Id.

the private violence violated Israel's obligation to provide effective protection and remedies to victims of human rights violations (ICCPR Article 2(3); ICERD Article 6). The attack on the Palestinian children violated Israel's obligation under customary international humanitarian law to respect and protect children affected by armed conflict.

- On July 9, a settler from Nof Zion settlement opened fire on a group of Palestinian youths in front of a grocery store in East Jerusalem, shouting at them "leave."[91]

    - The settlers' shouts at Palestinians to "leave" violated Israel's obligations to condemn and eliminate racial discrimination (ICERD Article 2(1)(a), 2(1)(b)).

- On July 7, a group of Israelis attacked Muahmmed Abu Eid (42 years old) while he was at work in Jerusalem. The settlers beat his head with an iron pipe, causing severe injuries.[92]

- On July 10, a group of Israelis attacked Ali al-Dewani (41 years old), who works as a driver for Egged Buses. The settlers cursed at and beat Ali while he was working near the central station of West Jerusalem.[93]

    - The racially-motivated cursing violated Israel's obligations to condemn and eliminate racial discrimination (ICERD Article 2(1)(a), 2(1)(b)).

- On July 25, eight settlers attacked Amir Shubaki (20 years old) and Samer Mahfouz (20 years old) while they were walking in Beit Hanina near the Neve Yaakov settlement. One settler had asked Amir and Samer if they had a lighter to verify from their accent that they were Palestinian. The settlers surrounded Amir and Samer and beat them with sticks, wires, and metal devices. The attackers fractured Amir's nose and skull, causing him brain

---

91 Israeli settler 'shoots at Palestinians' in East Jerusalem, MA'AN NEWS AGENCY, July 8, 2014, Internet, http://www.maannews.net/eng/ViewDetails.aspx?ID=710831.

92 Weekly Report On Israeli Human Rights Violations in the Occupied Palestinian Territory (03 – 09 July 2014).

93 The Monthly Report on the Israeli Violations of Palestinian Rights in the Occupied City of Jerusalem July 2014, ARAB STUDIES SOCIETY – LAND RESEARCH CENTER, page 13.

and nerve damage, paralysis in his hand, and internal bleeding. Samer sustained severe bruises on his neck and shoulder. When the Israeli Security Forces arrived at the scene, they failed to call an ambulance. Instead, passerby Palestinians took them to the hospital.[94]

  - The settlers verified the victim's Palestinian identity before attacking him in this racially-motivated crime, in violation of Israel's obligations to condemn and eliminate racial discrimination (ICERD Article 2(1)(a), 2(1)(b)).

- On August 5, Israelis severely beat Hisham Hassan Hasasneh (20 years old), a worker from the Bethlehem area, in Jerusalem.[95]

- On August 18, Israelis in a car attempted to run down a Palestinian near Wadi al-Joz Street.[96]

  - This attempted hit-and-run only violated the prohibition against inhuman treatment and willfully causing great suffering or serious injury to body or health under customary international law and Geneva Convention (IV) (Article 147).

- On August 26, seven settlers from the Ma'ale Mikhmas settlement, northeast of Jerusalem, attacked Raja'ei Ameen Barhoum (37 years old) while he was walking on the road. The settlers attacked him with a knife and an empty bottle and also threw stones at him. As a result of this attack, he was knocked unconscious and sustained cuts and bruises. A Palestinian driving by took him to the hospital for treatment.[97]

---

94 Weekly Report On Israeli Human Rights Violations in the Occupied Palestinian Territory (24 July – 03 August 2014), PCHR, Aug. 7, 2014, Internet, http://www.pchrgaza.org/portal/en/index.php?option=com_content&view=article&id=10645:weekly-report-on-israeli-human-rights-violations-in-the-occupied-palestinian-territory-24-july-03-august-2014-&catid=84:weekly-2009&Itemid=183.

95 Chris Carlson, 38 Palestinians Kidnapped in Jerusalem and West Bank, International Middle East Media Center (IMEMC), Aug. 5, 2014, Internet, http://www.imemc.org/article/68763.

96 The Monthly Report on the Israeli Violations of Palestinian Rights in the Occupied City of Jerusalem August 2014, Arab Studies Society – Land Research Center, page 16.

97 Weekly Report On Israeli Human Rights Violations in the Occupied Palestinian Territory (21 – 28 August 2014), PCHR, Aug. 28, 2014, Internet, http://www.pchrgaza.org/portal/en/index.php?option=com_content&view=article&id=10643:weekly-report-on-israeli-human-rights-violations-in-the-occupied-palestinian-territory-21-28-august-2014-&catid=84:weekly-2009&Itemid=183.

- On August 28, two Israelis attacked Ziad Musa al-Qawasmi (48 years old), a Palestinian taxi driver, while he was driving on one of the streets in Jerusalem. The two Israelis got into his taxi that night and asked him to take them to Bar Ilan Street. When he stopped the car so they could get out, one settler punched him in the face, fracturing his nose, while the other tried to strangle him. The perpetrators fled when a group of Israelis passed by.[98]

- On September 21, four Israelis armed with knives attacked and beat Muhammad Abdullah al-Tiryaqi (22 years old) near his house in Beit Hanina while he was returning from work. When the Israeli Security Forces arrived in a car at the scene, the perpetrators fled.[99]

- On October 17, Israelis attacked Faisal Muhammad Azzam (20 years old) in the Reinim Shalom hotel after he tried to defend a female colleague whom the perpetrators had verbally abused for wearing a hijab.[100]

- On October 31, an Israeli motorist deliberately ran down Yahya Ahmed Darwich (36 years old) when he was riding his motorcycle on Road 1 near the Sheikh Jarrah neighborhood.[101]

- On October 31, an Israeli motorist deliberately ran down Ali al-Sahwish (21 years old).[102]

- On November 18, 2014, four Israelis stabbed Fadi Jalal Radwan (22 years old) multiple times while he was walking in Kafr Aqab neighborhood, northern East Jerusalem. The perpetrators reportedly asked Fadi for a light before stabbing him in the legs

---

98 Weekly Report On Israeli Human Rights Violations in the Occupied Palestinian Territory (28 Aug. – 03 Sep. 2014), PCHR, Sept. 4, 2014, Internet, http://www.pchrgaza.org/portal/en/index.php?option=com_content&view=article&id=10627:weekly-report-on-israeli-human-rights-violations-in-the-occupied-palestinian-territory-28-aug-03-sep-2014&catid=144:new-reports.

99 Weekly Report On Israeli Human Rights Violations in the Occupied Palestinian Territory (18 – 24 September 2014), PCHR, Sept. 25, 2014, Internet, http://www.pchrgaza.org/portal/en/index.php?option=com_content&view=article&id=10659:weekly-report-on-israeli-human-rights-violations-in-the-occupied-palestinian-territory-18-24-september-2014-&catid=145:in-focus.

100 PCHR Report On Israeli Human Rights Violations in the oPt for 30 October – 29 November, 2014, IMEMC, Nov. 8, 2014, Internet, http://www.imemc.org/article/69645.

101 Id.

102 Id.

and back.[103]

i. Physical Attacks on Children

Each of the following incidents of private violence by Israeli civilians violated the prohibition against torture or cruel, inhuman or degrading treatment or punishment (ICCPR Article 7; CRC Article 37); the prohibition against inhuman treatment and willfully causing great suffering or serious injury to body or health under customary international humanitarian law and Geneva Convention (IV) (Article 147); and the obligation under customary international humanitarian law to respect and protect children affected by armed conflict.

- On July 3, an Israeli motorist deliberately ran down Adel Nabil Jouda (17 years old) near the Ramot settlement, north of Jerusalem. The attack broke his right leg and also resulted in bruises and wounds all over his body.[104]

- On August 7, an Israeli threw stones at Ritaj Ra'ed al-Hantouli (16 months) while she was with her family in front of their house in the Bab al-Magharba area south of the Old City. She sustained bruises and cuts to her leg as a result of this attack. The Israeli Security Forces were present in the area when the perpetrator threw the stones but took no action.[105]

- On August 9, three Israelis in a car verbally abused and attempted to run down 'Ola 'Olayan while she was returning from school to her home in Beit Safafa, southern East Jerusalem. The perpetrators attempted to run her over on Al-Tantour Street, as she walked from the school bus to her home.[106]

---

103 Palestinian stabbed by Israelis in northern Jerusalem, Ma'an News Agency, Nov. 19, 2014, Internet, http://www.maannews.net/eng/ViewDetails.aspx?ID=740907.

104 Weekly Report On Israeli Human Rights Violations in the Occupied Palestinian Territory (03 – 09 July 2014).

105 Weekly Report On Israeli Human Rights Violations in the Occupied Palestinian Territory (07 – 13 August 2014), PCHR, Aug. 14, 2014, Internet, http://www.pchrgaza.org/portal/en/index.php?option=com_content&view=article&id=10588:weekly-report-on-israeli-human-rights-violations-in-the-occupied-palestinian-territory-07-13-august-2014-&catid=84:weekly-2009&Itemid=183.

106 Id.

- This attempted hit-and-run only violated the prohibition against inhuman treatment and willfully causing great suffering or serious injury to body or health under customary international law and Geneva Convention (IV) (Article 147) and the obligation under customary international humanitarian law to respect and protect children affected by armed conflict. The use of racist insults violated Israel's obligations to condemn and eliminate racial discrimination (ICERD Article 2(1)(a), 2(1)(b)) and incitement to racial discrimination (ICERD Article 4).

- On September 25, an Israeli in a car deliberately ran down Adam Ali al-Rasheq (10 years old) in Silwan, south of the Old City, near Adam's family home. Witnesses called the Israeli Security Forces; however, the Israeli Security Forces never showed up.[107]

List of Named Victims

1. Ali Ahmed Abu Samra, 30
2. Ahmed al-Sabbagh, 24
3. Mahmoud al-Sabbagh, 19
4. Muahmmed al-Shawish, 20
5. Muahmmed Abu Eid, 42
6. Ali al-Dewani, 41
7. Amir Shubaki, 20
8. Samer Mahfouz, 20
9. Hisham Hassan Hasasneh, 20
10. Raja'ei Ameen Barhoum, 37
11. Ziad Musa al-Qawasmi, 48

107 Weekly Report On Israeli Human Rights Violations in the Occupied Palestinian Territory (25 September – 01 October 2014), PCHR, Oct. 2, 2014, Internet, http://www.pchrgaza.org/portal/en/index.php?option=com_content&view=article&id=10669:weekly-report-on-israeli-human-rights-violations-in-the-occupied-palestinian-territory-25-september-01-october-2014-&catid=84:weekly-2009&Itemid=183.

12. Muhammad Abdullah al-Tiryaqi, 22

13. Faisal Muhammad Azzam, 20

14. Yahya Ahmed Darwich, 36

15. Ali al-Sahwish, 21

16. Fadi Jalal Radwan, 22

17. Adel Nabil Jouda, 17

18. Ritaj Ra'ed al-Hantouli, 16 months

19. 'Ola 'Olayan, school-aged

20. Adam Ali al-Rasheq, 10

c. Attempted Kidnappings

Each of the following incidents of private violence by Israeli civilians violated the prohibition against inhuman treatment and willfully causing great suffering or serious injury to body or health under customary international humanitarian law and Geneva Convention (IV) (Article 147).

Israel is responsible for the following incidents because the impunity with which the perpetrator(s) committed violence against Palestinian(s) indicates that Israel acknowledged and adopted the private conduct as its own.

- On July 3, three Israelis attempted to kidnap Ammar Abu Asbeh (46 years old) near Shaftai Israel Street in Jerusalem. As Ammar walked in the area, three Israelis in a car stopped him and asked to see his identification card, which he refused to produce. The perpetrators forced him into the car. Ammar managed to escape by opening the car door and jumping out.[108]

108 Chris Carlson, Soldier and Settler Violence Continues Across West Bank, IMEMC, July 4, 2014, Internet, http://www.imemc.org/article/68327Ibrahim.

- On August 31, three Israelis tried to kidnap Ahlam Awad Muhei Awadallah (26 years old) while she was returning to her house in Al-Sahel quarter in Shuafat. The Israelis were in a car and cursed at her and tried to pull her into the car, but nearby Palestinian residents were able to stop her abduction.[109]

i. Attempted Kidnappings of Children

Each of the following incidents of private violence by Israeli civilians violated the prohibition against torture or cruel, inhuman or degrading treatment or punishment (ICCPR Article 7; CRC Article 37); the prohibition against inhuman treatment and willfully causing great suffering or serious injury to body or health under customary international humanitarian law and Geneva Convention (IV) (Article 147); and the obligation under customary international humanitarian law to respect and protect children affected by armed conflict.

- On June 30, a settler from Adam settlement and his two 16-year-old Israeli accomplices attempted to kidnap Mousa Rami Zaloum (9 years old) when he was walking with his mother in Shuafat neighborhood, northern East Jerusalem. While they were walking on the main street, an Israeli tried to strangle Mousa and put him into a car driven by another Israeli. Mousa's mother hit one of the perpetrators on the head repeatedly with her cell phone, after which two Israelis severely hit her chest and head before fleeing. The Israeli Security Forces did not respond to this incident.[110]

- On July 3, four settlers from the Pisgat Zeev settlement entered the Al-Samah quarter of Beit Hanina neighborhood and attempted to kidnap Mohammad al-Kiswani (7 years old). However, Palestinians heard Mohammad's screams and prevented his abduction. The settlers were able to flee under the protection of ISF personnel, who temporarily detained two Palestinians as they pursued the perpetrators of the attempted kidnapping.[111]

---

109 Weekly Report On Israeli Human Rights Violations in the Occupied Palestinian Territory (28 Aug. – 03 Sep. 2014).

110 Itamar Sharon, Abu Khdeir murder suspect gives chilling account of killing Read more: Abu Khdeir murder suspect gives chilling account of killing, The Times of Israel, Aug. 12, 2014, Internet, http://www.timesofisrael.com/we-said-they-took-three-of-ours-lets-take-one-of-theirs/; Weekly Report On Israeli Human Rights Violations in the Occupied Palestinian Territory (26 June – 02 July 2014).

111 Weekly Report On Israeli Human Rights Violations in the Occupied Palestinian Territory (03 – 09 July 2014).

- On July 28, two settlers attempted to kidnap Taha Riad Tufaha (2 years old) while he was walking with his family in Shuafat neighborhood. One settler grabbed the boy and tried to run away with him, but his family and other Palestinians rescued him. The settlers escaped in a car driven by a female settler and drove towards Ramot settlement. ISF personnel came to the site, but did not identify or locate the perpetrators.[112]

- During the week of July 22–August 4, settlers made three failed attempts to kidnap children, including a four-year-old child.[113]

- On August 20, Israelis attempted to kidnap a Palestinian child in Beit Hanina.[114]

- On September 24, eight Israelis attempted to kidnap Muhammad Khaled al-Zaghal (11 years old) while he was walking near Al-Juthmanya church near Lion's Gate of the Old City. The perpetrators chased the child, but he managed to escape and hide in a Palestinian car. When the Israeli Security Forces arrived, they arrested the child and claimed he threw stones at the Israelis.[115]

    - The arrest of this Palestinian child and blatant disregard for violence by Israeli civilians violated Israel's obligation to provide effective protection and remedies to victims of human rights violations (ICCPR Article 2(3); ICERD Article 6).

- On October 12, an Israeli attempted to kidnap Majed Majed Hazina (4 years old) from the entrance of his house in Al-Sa'diya neighborhood of the Old City. However, some Palestinian youths prevented the Israeli from abducting the boy. The boy's mother went to the police station and asked the Israeli Security Forces to

---

112 Weekly Report On Israeli Human Rights Violations in the Occupied Palestinian Territory (24 July – 03 August 2014)

113 Protection of Civilians Two-Week Reporting Period: 22 July – 4 August 2014, U.N. Office for the Coordination of Humanitarian Affairs occupied Palestinian territory (OCHA oPt), Page3, Internet, http:// www.ochaopt.org/documents/ocha_opt_protection_of_civilians_weekly_report_2014_8_08_english.pdf.

114 Patrick Strickland, Palestinians 'suffocating' in Jerusalem, Al Jazeera, August 28, 2014, Internet, http://www.aljazeera.com/news/middleeast/2014/08/palestinians-jerusalem-attacks-israel-gaza-20148258042106687.html.

115 Weekly Report On Israeli Human Rights Violations in the Occupied Palestinian Territory (18 – 24 September 2014).

arrest the perpetrator, but her request was denied.[116]

- The blatant disregard for the private violence violated Israel's obligation to provide effective protection and remedies to victims of human rights violations (ICCPR Article 2(3); ICERD Article 6).

List of Named Victims

1. Ammar Abu Asbeh, 46
2. Ahlam Awad Muhei Awadallah, 26
3. Mousa Rami Zaloum, 9
4. Mohammad al-Kiswani, 7
5. Taha Riad Tufaha, 2
6. Muhammad Khaled al-Zaghal, 11
7. Majed Majed Hazina, 4

d. Destruction of Palestinian Property

Each of the following incidents of private violence by Israeli civilians, resulting in damage to Palestinian property, implicates Israel's obligations under Geneva Convention (IV) and customary international humanitarian law. Under Article 53 of Geneva Convention (IV), the Occupying Power is prohibited from destroying real and personal property without legitimate military necessity. The extensive destruction and appropriation of property, not justified by military necessity and carried out unlawfully and wantonly, is defined in Geneva Convention (IV), Article 147) as a grave breach.

Israel is responsible for the following incidents because the impunity with which the perpetrators committed violence against Palestinians indicates that Israel acknowledged and adopted the private conduct as its own.

- During the week of June 10, in one incident, settlers threw stones

116 Weekly Report On Israeli Human Rights Violations in the Occupied Palestinian Territory (02 – 15 October 2014), PCHR, Oct. 16, 2014, Internet, http://www.pchrgaza.org/portal/en/index.php?option=com_content&view=article&id=10677.

at Palestinian-owned vehicles, damaging cars near the Silwan neighborhood.[117]

- During the week of June 10–16, settlers bulldozed two dunums of uncultivated land in the Jerusalem village of An Nabi Samwil, which is located in the closed area between the separation wall and the Green Line.[118]

- On July 3, an Israeli was caught setting fire to many olive trees and fruit trees in Be'r al-Mishmisha. When the perpetrator attempted to flee, the people of Jabal al-Mukabbir caught him. The Israeli Security Forces arrived on the scene and took the perpetrator to the police station; however, he was released without further investigation.[119]

- On July 6, a group of Israelis smashed and slashed the tires of Salah Zubeida's car in Wadi al-Joz neighborhood while it was parked in front of his house.[120]

- During the week of July 8, settlers threw stones at Palestinian-plated vehicles driving on West Bank roads in East Jerusalem, damaging three of them.[121]

- On July 10, a settler threw a Molotov cocktail at Mustafa al-Salfiti's house in Aqbat Al-Saraya neighborhood of the Old City, damaging the house. Israeli settlers have seized several properties in Aqbat Al-Saraya over recent years and have used their presence to attack and harass Palestinian residents. The ISF are aware of this violence and harassment against Palestinians but protect the

---

117 Protection of Civilians Weekly Report 10 – 16 June 2014, U.N. OCHA oPt, Page 3, Internet, http://www.ochaopt.org/documents/ocha_opt_protection_of_civilians_weekly_report_2014_6_19_english.pdf.

118 Id.

119 The Monthly Report on the Israeli Violations of Palestinian Rights in the Occupied City of Jerusalem July 2014, Page 10.

120 Weekly Report On Israeli Human Rights Violations in the Occupied Palestinian Territory (03 – 09 July 2014).

121 Protection of Civilians Weekly Report 8 – 14 July 2014, U.N. OCHA oPt, Page 2, Internet, http://www.ochaopt.org/documents/ocha_opt_protection_of_civilians_weekly_report_2014_7_17_english.pdf.

perpetrator settlers.[122]

- On July 16, a group of settlers led by an extremist rabbi, Yehuda Glick, desecrated Al-Aqsa Mosque's courtyards under the protection of the Israeli Security Forces.[123]

- On August 13, a group of settlers from Adam settlement, north of Jerusalem, threw rocks at Palestinian cars near Jaba' junction, damaging many of them.[124]

e. Incitement to Racial Hatred and Discrimination

The following incidents of private violence by Israeli civilians involved explicit expressions of racial hatred and discrimination, which sometimes even constituted direct and public incitement to commit genocide by advocating for the killing of members of the Palestinian group (Genocide Convention Article 3(c)). This also violate Israel's obligations to condemn and eliminate racial discrimination (ICERD Article 2(1)(a), 2(1)(b)) and incitement to racial discrimination (ICERD Article 4).

Israel is responsible for the following incidents that incited and increased racial hatred and discrimination because settlers acted on the instructions of state actors in carrying out this type of conduct.

- On June 19, in two incidents, Israelis slashed the tires of and sprayed graffiti on 10 Palestinian cars in Beit Hanina.[125]

- On or about June 23, three masked Israelis dressed in black slashed the tires of at least 12 cars belonging to nine Palestinian families in the Al-Ashqairiya quarter of Beit Hanina. The perpetrators also wrote racist phrases on a school bus, including "Death to Arabs." The Palestinian families immediately informed the Israeli Security Forces, who showed up at the scene, photographed the cars, and documented the damage, but took no further action to

122 The Monthly Report on the Israeli Violations of Palestinian Rights in the Occupied City of Jerusalem July 2014, Page 10.

123 Jewish settlers led by rabbi Yehuda Glick defile Aqsa Mosque, Occupied Palestine Blogging 4 Human Rights & Liberation of Palestine!, July 16, 2014, Internet, http://occupiedpalestine.wordpress.com/2014/07/16/jewish-settlers-led-by-rabbi-yehuda-glick-defile-aqsa-mosque/.

124 The Monthly Report on the Israeli Violations of Palestinian Rights in the Occupied City of Jerusalem August 2014, page 16.

125 Tires slashed in suspected racist attack, The Times of Israel, June 23, 2014, Internet, http://www.timesofisrael.com/tires-slashed-in-suspected-racist-attack/.

identify or apprehend the perpetrators.[126]

- On July 6, a group of Israelis accompanied by two ISF personnel smashed 10 cars and screamed revenge slogans in the Al-Tor neighborhood. A number of the perpetrators wore T-shirts that said "Death to Arabs."[127]

III. Excessive Use of Force by Israeli Security Forces in East Jerusalem

A. Protests in East Jerusalem During June-August 2014

Palestinian residents of East Jerusalem, particularly the youth, regularly protest to express opposition to the occupation and Israeli efforts to marginalize the Palestinian presence in the city. For Palestinians in East Jerusalem, who lack the civil and political rights of Israeli citizens, these protests are an essential avenue for demanding the fundamental rights that are systematically denied by the Israeli regime. The ISF routinely use unnecessary or disproportionate force to suppress Palestinian protests in East Jerusalem, further violating the rights of Palestinians under international law.

Between June and August 2014, the size and frequency of Palestinian protests in East Jerusalem escalated in response to Israel's 'Operation Protective Edge' in the West Bank, the kidnapping and murder of 16 year-old East Jerusalem resident Mohammad Abu Khdeir, and Israel's 'Operation Protective Edge' in Gaza. Palestinians staged protests across East Jerusalem to express their anger, sadness and frustration at Israel's violation of the rights of Palestinians throughout the oPt and the dehumanizing conditions of their own lives under Israeli occupation. Illustrating this wider context, a young Palestinian explained that:

---

126 Settlers vandalize 12 Palestinian cars in East Jerusalem, Ma'an News Agency, June 23, 2014, Internet, http://www.maannews.net/eng/ViewDetails.aspx?ID=707029.

127 Weekly Report On Israeli Human Rights Violations in the Occupied Palestinian Territory (03 – 09 July 2014).

> We went to the streets to fight back ... not just against settler violence, but to fight back to show them [the Israelis] that we Palestinians in Jerusalem are still alive, we're still breathing. ... We know they want to throw us all out of here, but we will continue to fight for our right to live in our city and our homeland.[128]

Over this period, there was a corresponding increase in the unnecessary or excessive use of force by the ISF against Palestinian demonstrators. The ISF employed sponge-tipped bullets, sound grenades, tear gas, skunk water and physical force in a disproportionate and wanton manner, with severe consequences. The ISF injured 453 Palestinian civilians between 2-7 July 2014, in the wake of Mohammed Abu Khdeir's murder.[129] On 3 July alone, over 200 Palestinians were injured in demonstrations throughout East Jerusalem.[130]

B. Israel's Obligations Regarding the Use of Force

1. International Humanitarian Law

As an occupying power, Israel has specific obligations to Palestinian civilians in East Jerusalem, who are 'protected persons' under international humanitarian law. The ISF's excessive use of force implicates the following obligations:

- Humane treatment: Protected persons shall at all times be humanely treated, and shall be protected especially against all acts of violence or threats thereof.[131] Measures of control and security should not affect the fundamental rights of the persons concerned, even in circumstances where a protected person

128 Interview by CCPRJ fieldworker, East Jerusalem, October 2014. The interviewee asked to remain anonymous for reasons of personal security.

129 United Nations Officer for the Coordination of Humanitarian Affairs (OCHA), Protection of Civilians Weekly Report 1 July - 7 July 2014 (11 July 2014) <http://www.ochaopt.org/documents/ocha_opt_protection_of_civilians_weekly_report_2014_7_11_english.pdf>.

130 Wadi Hilweh Information Center, Violent clashes in neighbourhoods and villages of Jerusalem (3 July 2014) < http://silwanic.net/?p=51031>.

is the legitimate object of strict measures dictated by military necessity.[132]

- Protection of life and property: While maintaining public order and safety, the individual lives and property of Palestinians must be respected.[133] Willful killings and the infliction of great suffering or serious injury to body or health to civilians are grave breaches of Geneva Convention (IV).[134] Such acts constitute war crimes and may be prosecuted under international criminal law.[135]

- Prohibition on collective punishment: The ISF is prohibited from imposing collective penalties on the protected population.[136] This draws upon a concept central to domestic law that a person cannot be punished for an offence that she or he has not committed.

2. International Human Rights Law

International human rights law applies to ISF acts in East Jerusalem and complements Israel's obligations under international humanitarian law.[137] Specifically, Israel is bound by the international standards for policing and law enforcement operations during public protests set forth in the International Covenant on Civil and Political Rights ('ICCPR'),[138] to which Israel is a party and which applies to all territory under Israel's effective

131 Geneva Convention (IV), art 27.

132 International Committee of the Red Cross (ICRC), Commentary - Art 27, Part III: Status and treatment of protected persons <https://www.icrc.org/applic/ihl/ihl.nsf/Treaty.xsp?documentId=AE2D-398352C5B028C12563CD002D6B5C&action=openDocument>.

133 Hague Regulations concerning the Laws and Customs of War on Land (18 October 1907) art 43, 46 ('Hague Regulations').

134 Geneva Convention (IV), art 147.

135 Rome Statute of the International Criminal Court, opened for signature 17 July 1998, 2187 UNTS 90 (entered into force 1 July 2002) art 8.

136 Geneva Convention (IV), art 33.

137 Legal Consequences of the Construction of a Wall in the Occupied Palestinian Territory (Advisory Opinion) [2004] ICJ Rep 136, paras 78, 86-113; Human Rights Committee, Concluding observations: Israel, UN Doc. (28 October 2014) para 5; Human Rights Committee, Concluding observations: Israel, UN Doc. CCPR/CO/78/ISR (5 August 2003) para 11.

138 International Covenant on Civil and Political Rights, opened for signature 16 December 1966, 999 UNTS 171 (entered into force 23 March 1976) ('ICCPR').

control, including the oPt.

- Freedom of Assembly, Opinion and Expression: The ISF must protect the rights of Palestinians to freedom of assembly as an integral avenue for expressing their opinions and grievances.[139] It must be reasonably expected that an assembly will be permitted, unless the requirements for limiting these rights listed in Article 19 and 21 are met.[140] But such limitations cannot be used as 'a cloak for the unreasonable restriction of political opposition' and all restrictive measures must be proportionate and necessary.[141]

- Right to Life: Israel has an absolute, non-derogable obligation to prevent the arbitrary deprivation of life.[142] This right to life demands that policing operations be carried out in a manner that minimizes the risk of death or serious injury.[143] It further demands that Israel undertake a bona fide investigation of any death or serious injury occurring during police operations, punish responsible security personnel, and provide compensation for violations to victims or their families.[144]

- International Policing Standards: The ISF's use of force must comply with accepted international policing standards to ensure that policing practices uphold and protect the right to life.[145] The key principles underlying these frameworks are that the use of force must always be a last resort and, if used, must strictly

---

139 ICCPR, art 19, 21; See also Frank La Rue, Report of the Special Rapporteur on the promotion and protection of the right to freedom of opinion and expression: Mission to Israel and the occupied Palestinian territory, Human Rights Council, 20th sess, Agenda Item 3, UN Doc A/HRC/20/17/Add.2 (11 June 2012) para 76.

140 Restrictions must be necessary to protect national security, public safety, public order, public health or morals or the rights and freedoms of others, see ICCPR, art 19, 21.

141 Adam McBeth, Justine Nolan and Simon Rice, The International Law of Human Rights (Oxford University Press, 2012) 104.

142 ICCPR, art 4(2); Human Rights Committee, General Comment No 6: Article 6, The Right to Life, 16th sess, UN Doc. CCPR/GEC/6630 (30 April 1982) para 3.

143 McCann and Others v United Kingdom (1995) Eur Court HR ; Gulec v Turkey (1998) IV Eur Court HR.

144 Human Rights Committee, Communication No 146/1983, UN Doc CCPR/C/24/D/146/1983 (4 April 1985) ('Baboeram v Suriname'); Human Rights Committee, Communication No 161/1983, UN Doc CCPR/C/31/D161/1983 ('Herrera Rubio v Columbia').

145 Code of Conduct for Law Enforcement Officials adopted by General Assembly resolution 34/169 (1979) ('Code'); Basic Principles for the Use of Force and Firearms by Law Enforcement Officials adopted by the Eighth UN Congress on the Prevention of Crime and the Treatment of Offenders (1990) ('Basic Principles').

adhere to the principles of proportionality and necessity.

G. Israeli Violations of Prohibitions on the Use of Excessive Force

1. Violent Suppression of Freedom of Assembly

The ISF violently suppressed and shut down the protests of Palestinian residents of East Jerusalem between June and August 2014, thereby violating their right to peaceful assembly under Article 21 of the ICCPR, and, as a consequence, their freedom of expression under ICCPR Article 19.[146] The ISF used excessive force to suppress protests in a blanket fashion as soon as they began and without sufficient grounds to justify the restrictions imposed on these rights.

Incidents of stone-throwing by Palestinian youth at these protests generally occurred in response to the ISF's use of force in violation of principles of proportionality and necessity, such as the arbitrary firing of rubber bullets and tear gas canisters into the crowd. Even in cases where Palestinian youth instigated confrontations with the ISF by throwing stones, the ISF were not justified in suppressing protests in their entirety. Individuals do not lose their right to freedom of assembly when there are sporadic and isolated violent outbreaks in the crowd.[147]

While States may take measures that derogate from these rights during times of public emergency, given the clear power differentials between the fully-armed ISF and Palestinian civilians, these protests cannot be said to have threatened the life and existence of Israel.[148] Thus, no derogation under Article 4 ICCPR to the rights protected by Articles 19 and 21 were permitted. Moreover, the measures employed by the ISF cannot be viewed as an aberration in times of public emergency, but rather constitute an

---

146 Violation of Article 21, will in most cases also result in the violation of Article 19, see Frank La Rue, Report of the Special Rapporteur on the promotion and protection of the right to freedom of opinion and expression: Mission to Israel and the occupied Palestinian territory, Human Rights Council, 20th sess, Agenda Item 3, UN Doc A/HRC/20/17/Add.2 (11 June 2012) para 76.

147 United Nations Human Rights Council, Report of the Special Rapporteur on Extrajudicial, Summary or Arbitrary Executions, Christof Heyns, (May 2008) UN Doc. A/HRC/17/28, p. 9.

148 ICCPR, art 4(1).

impermissible derogation under article 4 of the ICCPR, given that such measures involve discrimination on the basis of race, as part of routine discriminatory Israeli policing practices in relation to the Palestinian community. [149]

7. Excessive Use of Force Causing Serious and Lethal Injury

The ISF employed excessive force to suppress the protests in violation of Article 6 of the ICCPR, international policing standards, and international humanitarian law, as demonstrated by the following case studies.

a. Killing Of 16 Year-Old Mohammed Sunuqrut, Wadi al-Joz, 31 August 2014

Mohammad Sunuqrut, a 16 year-old Palestinian resident of East Jerusalem, died on 7 September 2014 due to injuries sustained on 31 August 2014, when Israeli Security Forces shot him in the head with a sponge-tipped bullet in the Wadi al-Joz neighborhood. An autopsy conducted at the Abu Kabir Forensic Institute confirmed that Mohammad died of a brain hemorrhage resulting from skull fractures caused by a projectile that was fired from less than 10 meters away.[150]

On the evening of 31 August 2014, Mohammad left his home in Wadi al-Joz to buy bread for his family. At approximately 8:15 pm, 28 year-old Ahmad Fua'd al-Tamimi was in his car about 10 meters from an intersection leading to the main street. He heard a gunshot close by and turned to the intersection where he saw Mohammad stumble backwards before falling to the ground. Ahmad began walking towards Mohammad but stopped about three meters away when six Israeli officers surrounded Mohammad. Ahmad asked the officers if he could come closer to Mohammad but they

---

149 ICCPR, art 4(1).

150 Nir Hasson, Palestinian teen killed by bullet to the head, despite Israeli police denial (12 September 2014) <http://www.haaretz.com/news/diplomacy-defense/.premium-1.615433>.

refused.[151] The Sunuqrut family's testimony supports this account:

> We went outside and found a group of soldiers surrounding him who were not giving him any help or support, and were not letting anyone give him support. Some people even say that they beat him. We tried to get through the surrounding soldiers to reach him, but we couldn't. My sister managed to get through...she saw the boy was bleeding, and then we pushed ourselves through and reached him.[152]

In a recorded telephone call to Magen David Adom (MDA), Israel's national emergency service, Ahmad can be heard saying that Mohammad "was shot in the head, he's unconscious," that Mohammd's head was swelling, and that he was bleeding and vomiting.[153] The Sunuqrut family further explained that:

> We tried to ask the soldiers to call the ambulance but nobody responded. Then we called the Red Crescent [a Palestinian ambulance service]...we discovered that somebody else had called an Israeli ambulance, but more than 15 minutes passed, and the ambulance didn't come.[154]

While Ahmad was on the phone with MDA, he asked where the ambulance was. The operator responded that it was at the entrance of Wadi al-Joz waiting for an Israeli police escort.[155] At approximately 8.35 pm, a Red Crescent ambulance arrived within 10 minutes of receiving a call and transferred Mohammad to Al-Makassed, a Palestinian hospital in East Jerusalem, while the Israeli ambulance never arrived. The Sunuqrut family recounted that:

---

151 Al-Haq, Palestinian Boy Dies Days after Being Shot with a Rubber-Coated Bullet by Israeli Forces < http://www.alhaq.org/documentation/weekly-focuses/858-palestinian-boy-dies-days-after-being-shot-with-a-rubber-coated-bullet-by-israeli-forces>.

152 Interview by CCPRJ field worker, November 2014. The interviewee asked to remain anonymous for reasons of personal security.

153 Nir Hasson, Palestinian teen killed by bullet to the head, despite Israeli police denial (12 September 2014) <http://www.haaretz.com/news/diplomacy-defense/.premium-1.615433>.

154 Excerpt from testimony to CCPRJ, November 2014.

155 Al-Haq, Palestinian Boy Dies Days after Being Shot with a Rubber-Coated Bullet by Israeli Forces < http://www.alhaq.org/documentation/weekly-focuses/858-palestinian-boy-dies-days-after-being-shot-with-a-rubber-coated-bullet-by-israeli-forces>.

> We went to Al-Makassed hospital...When we arrived they told us his situation was very critical...they called his father and brought him from work. The boy was in Makassed for one hour until we managed to take him to Hadassah hospital [an Israeli hospital in West Jerusalem]. The problem was that coordination between Makassed and Hadassah took time. We arrived in Hadassah by 12.00. The boy was injured at 8.15pm and didn't reach the operating room until 12.00...[156]

Mohammad was declared clinically dead at Hadassah Hospital on 4 September 2014 and legally dead on 7 September 2014.

The circumstances surrounding Mohammad's death indicate that the ISF deprived Mohammed of his life arbitrarily. The ISF failed to carry out their duties in a manner that minimizes the risk of death, in violation of Article 6 ICCPR and international policing standards, which stipulate that force can only be used when strictly necessary and to the extent required. It cannot be reasonably concluded that Mohammad, an unarmed Palestinian youth, was causing any threat or danger to the ISF or anyone else that could have justified the use of force. In those circumstances, using a firearm to shoot a sponge-tipped bullet to the head at close range indicates an extreme and wanton breach of the principles of proportionality and necessity, and constitutes an arbitrary killing.[157]

Moreover, the Israeli police initially refused the Sunuqrut family's request for an autopsy to determine the cause of death, falsely claiming that Mohammad was shot in the leg while throwing stones in a protest, causing him to fall and hit his head on the pavement.[158] They attempted to intimidate the Sunuqrut family into quietly burying Mohammad without an autopsy by calling members of the family into the police station for questioning. If the Israeli authorities fail to fairly investigate Mohammad's death and prosecute those found to be responsible – and their reluctance to conduct an autopsy suggests an unwillingness to conduct a bona fide investigation - this would constitute a further breach of Article 6 ICCPR.

---

156 Excerpt from testimony to CCPRJ, November 2014.

157 See Human Rights Committee, Communication 45/1979, UN Doc CCPR/C/15/D/45/1979 (31 March 1982) ('Suarez de Guerrero v Columbia').

158 Nir Hasson, Palestinian teen killed by bullet to the head, despite Israeli police denial (12 September 2014) <http://www.haaretz.com/news/diplomacy-defense/.premium-1.615433>.

The circumstances of Mohammad's killing are exceptional and point towards a willful killing, in grave breach of Geneva Convention (IV). According to witness accounts, Mohammad was alone, unarmed, and not near any clashes at the time he was shot. The autopsy concluded that Mohammad was shot from close range of less than 10 meters. This evidence provides no justification for any use of force against Mohammad, insofar as ISF personnel could not have reasonably believed that Mohammad was armed or otherwise posed a threat.

Furthermore, the evidence shows that the ISF breached their obligation to take immediate action to secure necessary medical care. The ISF's failure to provide medical care to Mohammad as he lay wounded in the street, the delay in ambulance services due to the ISF's failure to provide police escort to the MDA ambulance, and the difficulties associated in transferring Mohammad to a West Jerusalem hospital with the necessary facilities wasted critical time and may have contributed to Mohammad's death.[159]

b. Beating of 15 Year-Old Tareq Abu Khdeir, Shuafat, 3 July 2014

Tareq Abu Khdeir, a 15 year-old Palestinian who is also a United States citizen, was brutally beaten by three Israeli policemen on 3 July 2014 in Shuafat. This assault followed the kidnapping and murder of his 16 year-old cousin, Mohammed Abu Khdeir, on 2 July.

Tareq and several of his cousins were watching from an alley as ISF personnel confronted and shot rubber bullets at protesters. As the ISF moved towards the alley, Tareq began to run. He recounted that:

> I kept running a little further until the Israeli police grabbed me from behind, slammed my face into the floor, zip-tied my hands behind my back and started to kick me and punch me in the face and ribs. After they beat me, I fell unconscious ...then I woke up blindfolded in the jail.[160]

Tareq suffered severe injuries to his face, head and chest from the

159 Code, art 6.

160 See testimony of Tareq Abu Khdeir at C-SPAN, Israeli-Palestinian Conflict (1 August 2014) <http://www.c-span.org/video/?320809-1/discussion-israelpalestinian-conflict>.

beatings. This video recording of the incident shows two Israeli police arresting Tareq, with one handcuffing him while the other kicks and punches him repeatedly. A third policemen helps them drag Tareq, who appears to be unconscious, to another location.[161] Tareq was detained without medical treatment for six hours. He spent four days in jail without charge before being released on house arrest.

After pressure from United States officials and wide circulation of the footage online, a police investigation was launched, which led to one police officer being charged in the Jerusalem Magistrate's Court for assaulting a minor.[162] This charge is still pending.

The three ISF officers responsible for Tareq's brutal beating violated the right to bodily integrity embodied in the right to life, Article 6 ICCPR, as well as international policing standards, and the IHL duty to treat all protected persons humanely. The footage of the incident shows that Tareq was lying on the ground, already handcuffed, and posed no threat to the officers when the beating began.

c. Serious Injury of Tayseer Sandouka, Shuafat, 4 July 2014

Tayseer Sandouka, a 30 year-old Palestinian resident of East Jerusalem, was struck in the left eye by a sponge-tipped bullet, causing loss of sight, on 4 July 2014 in Shuafat, while attending the funeral of Muhammad Abu Khdeir.[163] Tayseer was already blind in his right eye, so this injury rendered him fully blind. He stated that:

> While participating in the funeral of Martyr Mohammad Abu Khdeir, the Israeli forces fired bullets that directly hit my eye, and only if you know which eye it hit. It hit my good eye. I am already half blind and only see with one eye and they just took it away from me.[164]

---

161 See footage at The Guardian, Palestinian TV shows alleged beating of Mohamed Abu Khdeir's cousin - video (6 July 2014) <http://www.theguardian.com/world/video/2014/jul/05/palestinian-tv-beating-of-mohamed-abu-khdeirs-cousin-video>.

162 Marissa Newman, Cop indicted for assult on US-Palestinian teen (10 September 2014) Times of Israel <http://www.timesofisrael.com/policeman-indicted-for-assault-on-us-palestinian-teen/>.

163 Association for Civil Rights in Israel, Police Violence Against East Jerusalem Residents (16 July 2014) <http://www.acri.org.il/en/2014/07/16/ej-police-violence/>.

Tayseer's debilitating injury is the consequence of the ISF's excessive use of force in their attempts to prevent East Jerusalem residents from using the funeral of Mohammed Abu Khdeir as a demonstration of Palestinian nationalism. In addition to violating international policing standards, the ISF also violated Israeli rules of engagement, which limit the use of sponge-tipped bullets to exceptional and extreme circumstances, where the target can be clearly identified, and only then targeting the lower body.[165] Many Palestinian civilians sustained severe head and upper-body injuries from sponge-tipped and rubber bullets over this period, indicating widespread breaches of Israeli rules of engagement.

d. Extrajudicial Killing of Mohammed Jabis, West Jerusalem, 4 August 2014

Mohammed Jabis, a 19 year-old Palestinian from the Jabal al-Mukabber neighborhood of oEJ, was shot and killed by the ISF on 4 August 2014 while working in an Orthodox Jewish neighborhood in West Jerusalem. At the time of his death, Mohammed was operating a tractor on a construction site in West Jerusalem. The ISF claim that Mohammed was killed while carrying out a terrorist attack. The ISF alleges that Mohammed deliberately ran over an Israeli man before ramming the tractor into the side of a public bus near the construction site, injuring several others. The ISF further alleges that it confronted and shot Mohammed as he fled the scene of the attack. Prime Minister Netanyahu award the ISF officer who killed Mohammed with a medal of service.

The Jabis family dispute this narrative. Rather, it believes that the incident was an accident caused by the Israeli killed in the incident, a resident of the Orthodox Jewish neighborhood who repeatedly harassed Mohammed at the construction site. Mohammed's uncle stated that:

> We are Palestinians and we are living under occupation in Jerusalem. So as you know, they [Israelis] always say that any accident, even if it is a traffic accident, is intentional when the person is Arab. So this is what happened to my nephew. He was working on a tractor...and there was a man, a religious Jewish

---

164 Wadi Hilweh Information Center, A rubber bullet injured Tayseer Sandouka in his eyes and causes him to lose sight (9 July 2014) <http://silwanic.net/?p=51188>.

165 Police regulations for controlling public order, section J(7)(a), (g), (j); See also Library of Congress, Police Weapons: Israel (September 2014) <http://www.loc.gov/law/help/police-weapons/israel.php>.

man who was there. He was walking around the tractor. The person responsible for the company told him [the religious Jewish man] many times, you should be aware of the tractor, the driver of the tractor can't see you.[166]

According to Mohammed's uncle, the Israeli was again harassing and intimidating Mohammed when the accident occurred. He claims that Mohammed's boss had previously warned the individual of the dangers of loitering at the construction site. Mohammed's uncle continued:

> So what do we think as the family of Mohammed? What happened was an accident. Maybe he shocked the man and he didn't see him, so he died. There were many religious Jewish people around. There was a school for religious Jews that was close to the situation there. They started shouting and throwing stones and saying bad words about Mohammed. So he is nineteen and a half years old, very young, I am sure that he was afraid, and he tried to escape from the situation, because it was dangerous to his life [as a Palestinian]. So he started driving, and he went to the main street. Before he reached the main street there were many Jews there who heard the shouting of the other Jews, and they started shooting at him [with firearms]. We counted the number of shots ... Mohammed was shot 47 times before he reached the bus. So he was injured and lost his control of the tractor... he tried to pass the bus but the street was very narrow, and it was very difficult to pass the bus. So he went in reverse and tried again, but they [the Israeli civilians] continued shooting at him. At this moment, he hit the bus, because he wanted to escape. But another person, a motorcyclist came from in front of Mohammed and the tractor, and started shooting at him. When he stopped [the tractor], he was alive, and we saw the cassette. And he made like this [a surrender sign] but the policeman shot him with two shots in his head. And this was his end... so what do we think? We are sure that everything happened as an accident, just an accident. They could have stopped him and investigated with him...when he stopped and raised his hands in surrender, they could have investigated him, but this is what happened...[167]

---

166 Interview by CCPRJ field worker, East Jerusalem, November 2014.

167 Id.

The Jabis family believes that Mohammed was shot by armed Israeli civilians after he accidentally ran over this individual, but before running the tractor into the bus.

Irrespective of whether the incident was an act of violence or an accident, the summary nature of Mohammed's killing is a clear violation of the right to life under Article 6 ICCPR. While state agents may use lethal force in limited circumstances, Article 6 requires that the level of force be proportionate to the circumstances.[168] In Mohammed's case, the ISF exercised lethal force arbitrarily, given that Mohammed was surrounded by security personnel and reportedly attempting to surrender. In adopting a 'shoot to kill' policy, the ISF usurped the judicial process to which Mohammed was entitled under Article 9 ICCPR. They did so without justification, as the circumstances show that the ISF could have easily apprehended Mohammed without killing him.

3. Collective Punishment of Palestinian Residents of Occupied East Jerusalem

a. Punitive House Demolitions

In early 2014, Israel reinstated its policy of punitive housing demolitions against Palestinians accused of security offenses. It increased its use of this unlawful practice after June 13, 2014.

Since 1967, Israel has demolished approximately 48,000 Palestinian homes in the oPt.[169] Punitive house demolitions were a consistent feature of the occupation until Israel suspended the practice in 1998, only to reinstate it in 2000, at the start of the second intifada.[170] Over the course of the second intifada, Israel conducted punitive demolitions of 664 Palestinian homes in the oPt.[171] The practice was suspended again in 2005 at the recommendation of an Israeli military committee, which found

---

168 Human Rights Committe, Communication No 45/1979, UN Doc CCPR/C/15/D/64/1979 'Suarez de Guerrero v Columbia').

169 Israel Committee Against House Demolitions, "Atavistic Violence: The Punitive Demolition of Palestinian Homes," Nov. 19, 2014, http://www.icahd.org/node/566.

170 Al-Haq, "Collective Punishment Policy Resumes: Israeli Punitive House Demolitions in the OPT," Dec. 8, 2014, http://www.alhaq.org/documentation/weekly-focuses/877-97collective-punishment-policy-resumes-israeli-punitive-house-demolitions-in-the-opt.

171 Id.

the practice ineffective in deterring acts of violence and euphemistically pronounced that it "walked the line" of legality.[172]
In 2014, Israel conducted at least 10 punitive house demolitions, displacing at least 28 Palestinians, including 6 children.[173] Among those demolished were the family homes of the alleged perpetrators of 12 June 2014 kidnapping and subsequent murder (these suspects were later killed rather than arrested and tried) and the home of Muhammad Jabis's mother in Jabal al-Mukabber.[174]

The policy of punitive home demolitions constitutes collective punishment of the Palestinian people in violation of Article 33 of Geneva Convention (IV) because the victims of the demolition – relatives of the suspected security offender, including women, the elderly and children – were not involved in the commission of any offence. In fact, the house demolition policy deliberately seeks to harm innocent civilians on the assumption that harming the relatives of Palestinian security offenders would deter others from carrying out such attacks.[175] In most cases, the suspect no longer resides in the home targeted for demolition because he is hiding from the ISF, is already in ISF custody, or was killed by the ISF, often in the course of the offense.[176] For example, on 19 November 2014, the family home of 20 year-old Abed al-Rahman a-Shaludi in Silwan was demolished. On 22 October 2014 Abed drove his car onto a Jerusalem light-rail platform in an alleged terrorist act, killing two people, including an infant.[177] Abed

---

172 B'Tselem, House Demolitions as Punishment: Background (26 November 2014) <http://www.btselem.org/punitive_demolitions>. Israel claims Regulation 119(1) of the Defense (Emergency) Regulations of 1945, enacted during the British Mandate, as the legal basis for punitive house demolitions, claiming that the Mandatory government's repeal of the emergency regulations at the end of the Mandate was ineffective because it was published in the Government Gazette in London but not the Palestine Gazette, and thus constituted an invalid "hidden law." The Israeli Supreme Court has upheld this position and has further ruled that the emergency regulations remained in effect throughout the period of Jordanian rule, such that they remained the law in force in the West Bank at the outset of the 1967 occupation, which IHL compels Israel, as the occupying power to respect. These positions have been roundly criticized. See David Kretzmer, The Occupation of Justice: The Supreme Court of Israel and the Occupied Territories (2002) 121-124.

173 Al-Haq, "Collective Punishment Policy Resumes," supra n. 170.

174 B'tselem, Order to demolish homes of Palestinians who perpetrated attacks unlawful and immoral (16 November 2014) <http://www.btselem.org/press_releases/20041116_planned_punitive_demolitions>.

175 B'Tselem, House Demolitions as Punishment: Background (26 November 2014) <http://www.btselem.org/punitive_demolitions>.

176 B'Tselem, House Demolitions as Punishment: Background (26 November 2014) <http://www.btselem.org/punitive_demolitions>.

177 Gili Cohen, Nir Hasson and Revital Hovel, Israel orders demolition of Jerusalem synagogue attackers' homes (20 November 2014) <http://www.haaretz.com/news/diplomacy-defense/.premium-1.627614>.

was shot and killed by the ISF as he fled the scene.[178] As a result of the demolition, nine innocent members of the Shaludi family, including three children, were left homeless.[179]

This punitive home demolition policy, which is applied only to Palestinians who commit security offenses against Jewish Israelis, clearly discriminates on the basis of race and/or national origin, in violation of Israel's obligations under international human rights law. Notably, the family homes of the three Jewish Israelis who confessed to the kidnapping and murder of Mohammed Abu Khdeir were not demolished.

b. Excessive Use of Force and Wanton Destruction of Property

Israel's excessive use of force and wanton destruction of property in suppressing the protests in East Jerusalem after June 13, 2014 additionally constitutes collective punishment of Palestinian residents of oEJ in violation of Article 33 of Geneva Convention (IV).

Two key features expose the ISF's conduct as collective punishment. First, the ISF's use of force extended to Palestinians not directly participating in the protests, including children and the elderly, resulting in serious injuries. On 1 August 2014, 14 year-old Alaa Hamdan was shot in the face by a sponge-tipped bullet while watching a confrontation between the ISF and local youth from her bedroom window inside her family's home in Issawiyeh. The confrontation occurred at least 10 meters away from her family home. Alaa was treated at Al-Makassed hospital and received twenty-five stitches to close the wound in her left cheek and jaw. She required continued hospital treatment for her wounds, which affected her vision in her left eye.[180] Other examples include the serious injury of 60 year-old year Aisha Hamdan, whose leg was broken by an ISF sound grenade while she was walking in Issawiyeh, [181] and a 9 year-old girl in Silwan who was injured by an ISF sponge-tipped bullet that was fired into

---

178 Peter Beaumont, Baby killed and eight wounded in suspected terror attack in Jerusalem (23 October 2014) <http://www.theguardian.com/world/2014/oct/22/jerusalem-attack-car-driven-light-rail-way-platform>.

179 Michael Schaeffer Omer-Man, Punitive home demolitions are racist - and just plain wrong (19 November 2014) <http://972mag.com/punitive-home-demolitions-are-racist-and-just-plain-wrong/98994/>; B'Tselem, House Demolitions as Punishment: Statistics (19 November 2014) <http://www.btselem.org/punitive_demolitions/statistics>.

180 Interview of the Hamdan family by CCPRJ field worker, East Jerusalem, November 2014.

181 Wadi Hilweh Information Center, The second day of the Martyrdom of the child Mohammad Abu Khdeir (4 July 2014) <http://silwanic.net/?p=51051>.

her house.[182]

Secondly, the ISF caused extensive damage Palestinian homes and vehicles in the vicinity of the protests. As indicated above, the ISF routinely shot sponge-tipped bullets into surrounding Palestinians homes, which caused property damage as well as serious injuries. Additionally, "skunk water," a foul-smelling liquid that causes irritation and redness in the eyes, skin irritation, abdominal pain, nausea and vomiting, was not only used to disperse protests but also sprayed indiscriminately across entire Palestinian neighborhoods.[183] The foul smell of skunk water lingers for days on persons, structures and entire neighborhoods.[184] On 6 July 2014, the entire neighborhood of Al-Tur was sprayed with skunk water from truck-mounted water canons.[185] The spray jets of the water canons are very powerful, with a range of 30-40 meters, and can cause major structural damage to properties and homes.[186]

8. Systematic Racial Discrimination in Use of Force by Israeli Security Forces

Israel's violations of international law in East Jerusalem during the relevant period occurred in the context of systematic racial discrimination in Israeli policies and practices in East Jerusalem. These policies and practices violate Articles 2 and 26 of the ICCPR, which prohibit any measures that discriminate on the basis of race. Some key examples of systematic racial discrimination by the Israeli authorities against Palestinians in East Jerusalem, and the manifestations of these policies and practices during the protests of June-August 2014, are outlined below.

---

182 Wadi Hilweh Information Center, Clashes break out in Jerusalem for the fifth day and the injury of a woman, a girl and a man in Silwan along with injuries with live bullets in Al-Ram (7 July 2014) < http://silwanic.net/?p=51156>.

183 The Association of Civil Rights in Israel (ACRI), Concerns of Excessive Use of Skunk Spray in East Jerusalem (10 August 2014) < http://www.acri.org.il/en/2014/08/10/skunk-ej/>.

184 B'tselem, Crowd Control: Israel's Use of Crowd Control Weapons in the West Bank (January 2013) 35-37; Material Safety Data Sheet (MSDS), Skunk: Repulsive odor liquid

< http://www.skunk-skunk.com/image/users/121755/ftp/my_files/MSDS_Skunk.pdf?id=3225191>

185 Wadi Hilweh Information Center, For the fourth consecutive day, clashes in the city of Jerusalem in support of Mohammad Abu Khdeir (6 July 2014) <http://silwanic.net/?p=51095>.

186 Ibid.

a. Crowd Control Mechanisms

It is widely documented that the ISF use harsher tactics and heavier weaponry to control Palestinian protests relative to demonstrations by Jewish Israelis. For example, the ISF reserve the use of rubber-coated metal bullets for use only in the oPt, excluding East Jerusalem.[187] Their use inside Israel was prohibited after the Or Commission, which investigated the ISF's killing of 13 Palestinian citizens of Israel in October 2000, recommended that rubber-coated metal bullets not be used as a means of crowd control given their inherent imprecision and lethal effects.[188] However, no such restrictions were imposed on ISF operations in the West Bank and Gaza Strip, where rubber-coated metal bullets are still regularly used against Palestinians.[189]

Similar discrimination in police tactics and weaponry apply between protests involving Palestinian residents of East Jerusalem and Jewish Israeli protestors. The ISF makes widespread use of sponge-tipped bullets, tear gas, sound grenades, skunk water and physical force against Palestinians in East Jerusalem.[190] In contrast, B'Tselem, an Israeli human rights NGO, has found that sponge-tipped bullets are not used in demonstrations with only Jewish Israeli participants.[191]

After the use of rubber-coated metal bullets was discontinued, the ISF began to substitute sponge-tipped bullets in Palestinian protests in East Jerusalem and Arab communities within Israel.
Sponge-tipped bullets have a black plastic base measuring 40mm in breach and 6.3cm in length with a blue, 30-gram foam nose that is designed to compress upon impact in order to reduce impact and damage. Sponge-tipped bullets are thus regarded as less dangerous than

---

187 B'tselem, Crowd Control: Israel's Use of Crowd Control Weapons in the West Bank (January 2013) 24-25; Al Haq, Repression of Non-Violent Protest in the Occupied Palestinian Territory: Case Study on the Village of Al-Nabi Saleh (2011) 29-31.

188 Adalah, The Official Summation of the Or Commission Report (September 2003)12-14, accessible at <http://adalah.org/features/commission/orreport-en.pdf>.

189 B'tselem, Crowd Control: Israel's Use of Crowd Control Weapons in the West Bank (January 2013) 25.

190 For an account of an Israeli protest in Tel Aviv over the same period, see Zafrir Rinat, In Tel Aviv, thousands protest against the Gaza operation (27 July 2014) < http://www.haaretz.com/news/national/1.607311>.

191 B'tselem, Crowd Control: Israel's Use of Crowd Control Weapons in the West Bank (January 2013) 43.

rubber-coated metal bullets.[192] However, as documented by B'Tselem, the manufacturer of the sponge-tipped bullets used by the ISF warns of the risk of death, serious injury and property damage, and thus recommends special training on their use.[193]

Israeli police regulations stipulate that the "impact on the torso [by sponge-tipped bullets] can be dangerous" and outline strict parameters for their use. Specifically, sponge-tipped bullets can only be used in situations where violence is directed towards police officers or other members of the public which may cause bodily injury or property damage. Even then, they may only be used if less severe methods have been exhausted and if their use is necessary and proportionate.[194]

During the protests in East Jerusalem between June-August 2014, the ISF used a larger and heavier model of sponge-tipped bullet that inflicts more grave bodily harm.[195] This new model is black rather than blue, denser, and double the weight: 62 grams, compared to the 30-gram blue model.[196] Dr. Amin Abu Ghazeleh of the Palestinian Red Crescent Society in Jerusalem stated that "anyone shot by this bullet suffers an open wound and if it hits the head from a short distance, it could cause brain damage."[197] While the ISF collected and removed the projectile that hit Mohammad Sunuqrut, the gravity of his injuries and consequent death suggests that he may have been struck by this heavier sponge-tipped bullet. Mohammad's death further calls into question whether the use of sponge-tipped bullets may accurately be categorized as a non-lethal crowd control method.

---

192 Id.

193 Id. at 44.

194 Procedure for the Use of 40mm Sponge Rounds in Disturbances of the Peace, Appendix B, sections 1-5 [in Hebrew]. For further discussion, see B'tselem Crowd Control: Israel's Use of Crowd Control Weapons in the West Bank (January 2013) 43-45

195 Nir Hasson, Sources: Palestinian teen killed by bullet to hear, despite Israeli police denial (12 September 2014) <http://www.haaretz.com/news/diplomacy-defense/.premium-1.615433>.

196 Nir Hasson, Sources: Palestinian teen killed by bullet to hear, despite Israeli police denial (12 September 2014) <http://www.haaretz.com/news/diplomacy-defense/.premium-1.615433>. See also Mairav Zonszein, Autopsy contradicts police, shows Palestinian teen was shot in the head (12 September 2014) <http://972mag.com/autopsy-contradicts-police-shows-palestinian-teen-was-shot-in-head/96634/>, in particular note the photograph of the Dr. Rafik Husseini, Director of Al-Makassed Hospital in East Jerusalem, holding the new crowd control projectile.

197 Nir Hasson, Sources: Palestinian teen killed by bullet to hear, despite Israeli police denial (12 September 2014) <http://www.haaretz.com/news/diplomacy-defense/.premium-1.615433>.

B. Investigations and Indictments of ISF Personnel

The impunity of ISF personnel for using unjustified or excessive force against Palestinians has been widely documented by Israeli human rights NGOs, including Yesh Din and B'Tselem. These organizations have concluded that the ISF are not capable of conducting independent, fair and professional investigations into offenses committed by ISF personnel against Palestinians.[198] Yesh Din's data for 2013 indicates that while 199 of the 236 complaints of ISF personnel offences against Palestinian persons or property in the oPt were investigated, indictments were issued in only six of these cases.[199] Between 2010-2013, only 1.4 percent of Palestinian complaints against ISF personnel resulted in an indictment.[200] This effective impunity for human rights violations committed by ISF personnel against Palestinians amounts to systematic racial discrimination in violation of Articles 2 and 26 ICCPR.

This culture of impunity extends to ISF violence against Palestinians in East Jerusalem, as illustrated by the experience of the Sunuqrut family. The Israeli police initially refused to conduct an autopsy on Mohammad Sunuqrut, reportedly encouraged the family to decline an autopsy, and retaliated against the family for demanding an autopsy by investigating family members. One member of the Sunuqrut family summed up the family's frustration and disillusionment with the Israeli authorities:

Every time there is an injustice against Palestinians, they [the Israelis] play with the facts...Anybody they want to arrest, they shoot to kill...If you are a Palestinian in Jerusalem, you are a target. We Palestinians should always follow the facts and seek justice. Even though it is their law [the Israelis]. Even through the judge is the oppressor, and we have no faith in the Israeli legal system.[201]

---

198 Yesh Din, Israeli human rights organisations B'tselem and Yesh Din: Israel is unwilling to investigate harm caused to Palestinians (9 August 2014) < http://www.yesh-din.org/postview.asp?postid=283>.

199 Yesh Din, Law Enforcement upon IDF Soldiers in the Occupied Palestinian Territory: Figures for 2013 (September 2014) 1.

200 Yesh Din, Law Enforcement upon IDF Soldiers in the Occupied Palestinian Territory: Figures for 2013 (September 2014) 7.

201 Personal interview with the Sunuqrut family, CCPRJ, November 2014.

c. Access to Emergency and Medical Services

The circumstances surrounding Mohammed Sunuqrut's death also highlight the systematic racial discrimination in Israel's emergency and medical service policies in East Jerusalem.

Magen David Adom (MDA), Israel's national emergency service, was called to respond to Mohammed's critical condition. Within nine minutes of receiving the call, the MDA ambulance arrived at the entrance of the Palestinian neighborhood of Wadi al-Joz, but it never reached the scene. Israeli policy stipulates that any ambulance or medical team requires a police escort to enter a Palestinian neighborhood during a 'security situation' to prevent harm to Israeli medical personnel. The police escort never arrived and the MDA ambulance was unable to proceed.[202]

After 15 minutes of waiting for the MDA ambulance to arrive, the Sunuqrut family contacted the Palestinian Red Crescent Society (PRCS), which dispatched an ambulance that arrived at the scene within 10 minutes and transported Mohammed to Al-Makassed, a Palestinian hospital in East Jerusalem. Given the delay of the MDA ambulance, Mohammad was left without proper medical assistance for approximately 20-25 minutes. Furthermore, Al-Makassed lacks the resources to provide the treatment that Mohammad required given his critical condition. Mohammad was picked up and taken to Al-Makassed by the PRCS ambulance at approximately 8:35pm. However, he was not transferred from Al-Makassed to Hadassah, an Israeli hospital in West Jerusalem, for nearly three hours. According to the Sunuqrut family, Mohammad did not reach the operating table at Hadassah until 12:00am.

Sunuqrut's case illustrates that Palestinians in East Jerusalem have inadequate access to health care resources in a discriminatory and largely-segregated health care system.[203] Israel has thereby failed its obligations under Article 2(2) and 12(1) ICESR, which requires States to create conditions, without discrimination, which ensure "all medical service and medical attention."

202 Nir Hasson, Police, Protesters clash after funeral of East Jerusalem teen (9 September 2014) < http://www.haaretz.com/news/national/.premium-1.614799>.

203 Nir Hasson, Police, Protesters clash after funeral of East Jerusalem teen (9 September 2014) < http://www.haaretz.com/news/national/.premium-1.614799>.

International policing standards and IHL also articulate positive obligations for ISF personnel to respect and protect the transport of sick or injured civilians to hospital.[204]

V. Arrests, Detentions and Home Invasions

Israeli security forces have a history of arresting Palestinians in the oPt and Palestinian citizens of Israel in order to stifle their freedom of expression, right of assembly, and participation in political life. These arrests violate Israel's obligations under IHRL to uphold freedom of expression, freedom from arbitrary arrest, and nondiscrimination in the protection of human rights. They further violate the IHL prohibition on unlawful confinement. The conditions of detention after arrest also violate relevant IHL and IHRL standards.

Between 2 July and 8 August, the ISF arrested 1,471 protestors across Israel and occupied East Jerusalem on charges of disturbing public order, unlawful gatherings, rioting and violence against people and property.[205] From these arrests, more than 650 criminal investigations were opened and more than 350 people were charged.[206] Although most of the persons arrested for attacking demonstrators were right-wing Jewish Israelis, not a single Jewish Israeli was charged with a crime.[207] Quite simply, "Arabs are charged, Jews aren't."[208] In East Jerusalem, 750 Palestinians were arrested, including 250 children, between July and October 2014.[209]

A. Stifling Free Expression and Assembly By Arbitrary and Discriminatory Arrests

Israel systematically suppresses Palestinian freedom of expression and assembly in East Jerusalem by delaying and denying protest permits, using excessive force, and making arbitrary arrests. These practices violate a host of rights protected by IHRL and IHL.

204 Code, Article 6; Geneva Convention (IV), Article 21.

205 The Israel Police's War Against Arab Protesters, Haaretz, 16, August 2014.

206 Id.

207 Id.

208 Id.

209 The National, Israel Targets Teens, Children in Protester Crackdown, October 8, 2014.

1. Guarantees of Free Expression and Assembly

Freedom of expression and freedom of assembly are enshrined in various human rights documents, and are principles of customary international law. Article 13 of the Convention on the Rights of the Child (CRC) provides that the "child shall have the right to freedom of expression"[210] while Article 15 recognizes the child's right to "freedom of association and to freedom of peaceful assembly."[211] Article 21 of the ICCPR guarantees that the "right of peaceful assembly shall be recognized" by states parties while article 19 protects the right to freedom of expression.[212] The customary status of the rights to freedom of expression and assembly is reflected in Articles 19 and 20 UDHR, as well as various regional human rights treaties.[213]

2. Nondiscrimination in the Protection of Human Rights

Freedom of expression and assembly must be protected equally without regard to race/national origin, religion, or political opinion, among other protected classifications. This is a fundamental principle of international human rights law enshrined in article 5 of the International Convention on the Elimination of All Forms of Racial Discrimination[214] articles 2 and 4 of the ICCPR,[215] and article 2 of the Convention on the Rights of the Child.[216] It is also a fundamental rule of customary international law enshrined in national constitutions, and various international and regional human rights instruments, including article 2 of the Universal Declaration of Human Rights.[217] Further, it is a principle of international humanitarian

---

210 Convention on the Rights of the Child, article 13

211 Id., article 15.

212 ICCPR, article 19

213 European Convention on Human Rights, Art. 10; African Charter on Human and Peoples' Rights, Art. 9; American Convention on Human Rights, Art. 13, ASEAN Human Rights Declaration, Art. 23

214 CERD, article 5.

215 ICCPR, articles 2 and 4.

216 CRC, article 2.

217 UDHR, article 2.

law protected by art. 13 and 27 of the IV Geneva Convention.[218]

B. ISF Arrests and the Denial of Free Speech

Israel uses its permit regime governing protests and rallies to stifle opposition from Palestinian citizens of Israel, Palestinians in East Jerusalem, and even liberal Jews. [219] But whereas Jewish protesters are occasionally arrested, briefly detained and released, Palestinian protesters are confronted with far greater force, arrested in far greater numbers, and detained far longer.[220]

Israel's suppression of free speech included a troubling attack on press freedom. On 6 June, Israeli security forces broke into the East Jerusalem offices of Palmedia, allegedly for operating without a license, and halted the airing of "Good Morning Jerusalem," a live weekly television program.[221] The program's producer, Nader Biebars, cameraman Ashraf Shwaiki, and program guest Ala'a al-Haddad, a member of the Prisoners' Families Committee in Jerusalem, were all arrested, ironically, during a segment focusing on Israeli human rights violations against Palestinian prisoners."[222]

1. Guarantees of Freedom from Arbitrary Arrest

The right to freedom from arbitrary arrest is enshrined in various human rights treaties and is recognized as a principle of customary international law. Article 9 of the ICCPR provides that "no one shall be subjected to arbitrary arrest or detention."[223] Likewise, CRC Article 37 establishes that

218 IV Geneva Convention, articles 13 and 27. https://www.icrc.org/applic/ihl/ihl.nsf/Article.xsp?action=openDocument&documentId=DC3ED5AE9C6F7419C12563CD0051BAA4

219 http://www.aljazeera.com/news/middleeast/2014/08/israel-palestinians-anti-war-protesters-gaza-2014839155862548.html

220 http://www.haaretz.com/opinion/.premium-1.612231

221 Applied Research Institute of Jerusalem, Israeli Violations of Palestinian Rights in the Occupied City of Jerusalem during the month of June 2014

222 Id.

223 ICCPR, article 9.

no child is to arbitrarily be deprived of liberty.[224] Its customary status is reflected in Article 9 UDHR and regional human rights treaties.[225] Freedom from arbitrary arrest is also guaranteed in IHL by Article 78 of Geneva Convention (IV), which allows the detention of protected persons only for "imperative reasons of security," and Common Article 3 to the Geneva Conventions, insofar as arbitrary deprivation of liberty is incompatible with its requirement of humane treatment.[226] Its status as customary IHL is reflected in the military manuals of more than 70 states.[227]

The Human Rights Committee clarified the meaning of arbitrary arrest and detention in its General Comment 35 on liberty and security of person. In addition to explaining that any arrest without legal basis is arbitrary,[228] the Human Rights Committee noted:

> arrest or detention may be authorized by domestic law and nonetheless be arbitrary... "[A]rbitrariness" is not to be equated with "against the law", but...inappropriateness, injustice, lack of predictability, and due process of law,[229] as well as elements of reasonableness, necessity, and proportionality.[230]

Further, freedom from arbitrary arrest must be protected equally regardless of race, religion, language, national origin or political opinion.[231]

2. Israeli Violations of Freedom from Arbitrary Arrest and Detentions

224 CRC, article 37.

225 American Convention on Human Rights, Article 7; ASEAN Human Rights Declaration, Article 12; European Convention on Human Rights, Article 5; African Charter on Human and Peoples' Rights, Article 6.

226 IV Geneva Convention, article 78.

227 ICRC, Customary International Humanitarian Law, Rule 99, Deprivation of Liberty.

228 Human Rights Committee, General Comment No. 35 (Advance Unedited Version) ¶ 11.

229 1134/2002, Gorji-Dinka v. Cameroon, ¶ 5.1; 305/1988, Van Alphen v. The Netherlands, ¶ 5.8.

230 Human Rights Committee General Comment 35, ¶ 12.

231 ICCPR Art. 9 in conjunction with article 2, CRC article 37 in conjunction with art. 2, UDHR Art. 9 in conjunction with article 2.

While Palestinians throughout the oPt, including East Jerusalem, are always subject to arbitrary arrest, such arrests surged following the death of Mohammad Abu Khdeir.[232] In some cases, Palestinians were arrested simply for organizing protests.[233] Dov Khenin, a Jewish Israeli MP from the left-wing Hadash party, observed:

> most of the detainees were arrested for attending protests. Those who threw stones and should stand trial for violence fled. Those who were arrested were apprehended because they stood around and didn't run.[234]

Noting the large number of those arrested for assaulting the police, Khenin said, "you would think that the hospitals are full of wounded cops, and I don't remember there being any."[235] Indeed, in many cases of these arrests, the Israeli authorities have presented no evidence aside from the arresting officer's word.[236]

In that regard, Israeli security forces have a history of fabricating excuses for arresting demonstrators who have not thrown stones or engaged in violent activity. During a demonstration in the West Bank town of Bil'in, Israeli security forces arrested protestors after stones were thrown at Israeli security forces. Protest organizers insisted that undercover Israeli officers threw the stones to create a pretext for arresting protesters. However, it was not until the trial of one of the protestors, Arab Israeli MP Mohammed Barakeh, that the undercover officers actually testified that they had, in fact, started the stone-throwing at the protests.[237] Undercover Israeli security officers reportedly infiltrated protests in East Jerusalem during the relevant period.[238]

---

232 See, e.g., Al Jazeera, Israel accused of cracking down on lawyers, 14 May, 2014 (discussing the arrest of human rights lawyers in East Jerusalem); Samidoun, Israeli Occupation Forces Re-arrest Ayman Nasser, Legal Unit Coordinator at Addameer Prisoner Support and Human Rights Association, 18 September, 2014, (discussing the arrest of another rights activist), Human Rights Committee, Concluding observations on the fourth periodic report of Israel, par. 19.

233 972 Magazine, Following wave of protests, Israel arrests scores of Arab activists, minors, 23 July, 2014

234 Haaretz, Israel Police's war against Arab protesters, 16, August, 2014.

235 Id.

236 Al Jazeera, Israel cracks down on anti-war protesters, 5 August, 2014.

237 972 Magazine, Commander admits: Undercover Israeli officers threw stones at soldiers in Bil'in, 7 May, 2012.

238 See, e.g., Maan News Agency, Palestinians clash with Israeli troops across East Jerusalem, 23 July 2014.

In the aftermath of the Muhammad Abu Khdeir's murder, the ISF arrested up to 30 members of the Abu Khdeir clan.[239] Tareq Abu Khdeir, Muhammad's cousin, was brutally beaten and arrested by the ISF on 5 July while watching a protest in East Jerusalem.[240] Although the police officer who beat Tareq alleges that he feared for his life because the 15 year-old would not release a slingshot,[241] video footage of the incident shows the officer repeatedly kicking Tareq in the head while his hands were cuffed behind his back.[242] No slingshot is visible in any of the footage.[243] Tareq's uncle, Issa Abu Khdeir, was arrested and detained for five days for allowing Tareq to give media interviews from his Shuafat home.[244] Other family members were arrested on equally frivolous grounds. Mohammad Jaser Abu Khdeir, a dentist, was arrested for providing emergency medical care at a violent protest.[245] As explained by Hana Abu Khdeir, a 43-year-old mother of two, the Israeli authorities "want to calm us down because our kid got killed...Controlling Abu Khdeir means controlling Shuafat."[246]

These arrests are both arbitrary because of their "inappropriateness, injustice, lack of predictability"[247] and an expression of collective punishment in violation of Article 33 of the IV Geneva Convention.[248]

---

239 Washington Post, Slayings, protests, arrests vex Palestinian clan with strong U.S. ties, 2 September, 2014.

240 Mondoweiss, Tariq Abu Khdeir is not deterred: Despite Israeli police attack, he plans on returning to Palestine, 19 August, 2014.

241 Times of Israel, Cop who beat US-Palestinian teen says he felt his life was in danger, 28 September, 2014.

242 Youtube, Israeli police beating Palestinian in Shuafat, Jerusalem, 3 July 2014, available at https://www.youtube.com/watch?v=0Aaj0YM45t4#t=46, and Youtube, Israel police beat American teen Tarek Khdeir available at https://www.youtube.com/watch?v=JhFa_kgB1cc

243 Id.

244 McClatcheyDC, Palestinian family possibly 'singled out for arrest' by Israel, U.S. says, 28 August, 2014.

245 Id.

246 Jewish Daily Forward, Sprawling Abu Khdeir Family Spreads Deep Roots in Jerusalem — and U.S., 2 September, 2014.

247 Human Rights Committee General Comment 35 ¶ 11.

248 IV Geneva Convention, article 33.

3. Discrimination in Protecting the Freedom from Arbitrary Arrest

Following the 1967 War, Israel fully extended its laws to occupied East Jerusalem, an act recognized by the international community as an illegal annexation.[249] Thus, Palestinians in East Jerusalem are subject to Israeli civil law. But whereas Jewish Israelis in Jerusalem are subject only to Israeli civil law and legal process, Palestinians Jerusalemites are subject to arrest and detention under three bodies of law: general Israeli criminal law; special Israeli laws pertaining to "security offenders," which are almost exclusively applied to Palestinians residents of East Jerusalem and Palestinian citizens of Israel; and the Israeli military orders that govern life in the oPt, if the Jerusalem resident's alleged offense was committed in, or has a connection with, other parts of the oPt.[250]

Adjudicating Palestinians in East Jerusalem under the military orders gives the Israeli authorities the power to order longer detentions with reduced judicial oversight and access to counsel.[251] Under the military judicial system, individuals may be detained for up to 8 days without appearing before a judge, 90 days without consulting a lawyer, and 188 days without being charged with a crime. These detention orders may be renewed indefinitely.[252] To hold Palestinian residents of East Jerusalem under military orders, the prosecution must show that the offense was committed in or otherwise has ties to other parts of the oPt. In practice, the prosecutor's burden in proving this connection is very slight, with arbitrary decisions taken to extend the interrogation period to its maximum limits.[253]

Further, Palestinian residents of East Jerusalem and Palestinian citizens of Israel are often classified as "security offenders," which also allows for longer periods of detention without charge than is allowed under general Israeli criminal law.[254] Security offenders can be detained up to 4 days before a court appearance, denied access to a lawyer for 21 days, and

---

249 See Section II(B)(2), supra.

250 Addameer, Forgotten City, Forgotten People: Jerusalemite Political Prisoners, the Oslo Process and a Struggle for Freedom 2011.

251 Id.

252 Israeli Military Order 1651.

253 id.

254 id.

held in custody without charge for 64 days.[255] In contrast, under Israeli civil law, suspects must be brought before a judge within 24 hours of arrest, allowed access to an attorney "without delay" and no later than 48 hours, and may remain in custody without charge for no more than 30 days.[256]

By subjecting Palestinians in East Jerusalem to this tripartite system of civil, security and military laws, while applying only Israeli civil law to Jewish citizens, Israel discriminates on the basis of religion and national origin in upholding the right to freedom from arbitrary arrest and detention. Israel thereby violates various IHRL obligations, including Article 2 of the ICCPR and Article 2 of the CRC, as well as its obligations under Articles 13 and 27 of Geneva Convention (IV).[257]

C. Transfer of Detainees from occupied East Jerusalem to Interrogation and Detention Centers Inside Israel

Article 49 of Geneva Convention (IV) prohibits the transfer of prisoners from occupied territory:

> Individual or mass forcible transfers, as well as deportations of protected persons from occupied territory to the territory of the Occupying Power or to that of any other country, occupied or not, are prohibited, regardless of their motive.[258]

While there is an exception to ensure the safety of the population or "imperative military reasons," transfer outside of the occupied territory is only allowed when "it is impossible to avoid such displacement."[259] If the text of Article 49's prohibition of transfer "regardless of…motive" were not clear enough, Article 76 makes it clear that this prohibition dictates that prisoners among the protected population shall serve their sentences within the occupied territory.[260] Article 147 of Geneva Convention (IV)

255 Criminal Procedure Law (Detainees suspected of security offenses) (Emergency Order) 2006.

256 Israel Criminal Procedure Law (Powers of Enforcement – Arrest), 1996.

257 Geneva Convention (IV), article 13 and 27.

258 Geneva Convention (IV), article 49.

259 Id.

260 Geneva Convention (IV), article 76.

makes the unlawful deportation, transfer, or confinement of a protected person a grave breach.[261]

Israel routinely flouts this fundamental rule of the law of occupation by transferring detainees from occupied East Jerusalem to the Russian Compound (Moskabiya) detention center in West Jerusalem.[262] Following the surge in arrests and detentions during the relevant period, detainees were transferred further outside occupied territory to Lod, Israel, because the Russian Compound was full.[263]

D. Torture

Torture is a grave breach of IHL and its prohibition is a preemptory norm of international law. Article 7 of the ICCPR states: "no one shall be subjected to torture or to cruel, inhuman or degrading treatment or punishment."[264] The prohibition of "torture and other ill-treatment has subsequently been incorporated into the extensive network of international and regional human rights treaties."[265] The UN Convention against Torture or Other Cruel, Inhuman or Degrading Treatment or Punishment ("CAT"), ratified by Israel, clearly spells out the obligation to eliminate torture.[266] It is also fundamental principle of customary international law as evidenced by various human rights treaties and state practice.[267]

Common Article 3 to the Geneva Conventions bans "violence of life and person, in particular murder of all kinds, mutilation, cruel treatment and torture" and "outrages upon personal dignity, in particular humiliating and degrading treatment." Article 31 of Geneva Convention (IV) states: "No physical or moral coercion shall be exercised against protected persons,

---

261 Geneva Convention (IV), article 147.

262 See, e.g., Al Akhbar English, Israeli forces detain four Palestinian children for throwing stones, 24 July, 2014; International Middle East Media Center, Six Palestinians, Including Two Children, Kidnapped In West Bank, Jerusalem, 17 September, 2014.

263 Maan News Agency, Jerusalem faces largest surge in arrests since 2nd Intifada, 27 August, 2014

264 ICCPR, article 7.

265 Human Rights Watch, The Legal Prohibition Against Torture, 11 March, 2003

266 Convention against Torture and Other Cruel, Inhuman or Degrading Treatment or Punishment

267 E.g. European Convention for the Protection of Human Rights and Fundamental Freedoms, the American Convention on Human Rights, and the African Charter on Human and Peoples' Rights.

in particular to obtain information from them or from third parties."[268]

However, in contravention of the prohibition against torture, and cruel and inhumane treatment, Israel routinely tortures detainees. Palestinian and Israeli human rights NGOs, including Defence for Children International (DCI) and Adalah, have found that Israeli investigators threatened detained Palestinian children with "beatings, isolation, torturing their fathers and raping their mothers and sisters" and that "children were denied food for dozens of hours unless they confessed to the charges against them."[269]

1. Noureddeen az-Zaghal

Noureddeen az-Zaghal, 17, from Abu Tor, was taken prisoner on July 6, 2014, after the soldiers stormed his family home after midnight. He was cuffed and blindfolded before the soldiers dragged him to their jeep, forcing him onto the vehicle's floor, face down, and beat him. Az-Zaghal was then moved to the al-Moskabiya interrogation center in Jerusalem, where he was interrogated and subjected to torture for 18 days. "I was then moved to the HaSharon prison; it is unfit for human use. It is very hot, with high humidity, and always overcrowded," he said, "The mattresses are filthy, torn and decayed. Bugs, worms and termites are all over the place."[270]

2. Mahmoud Abu Teir

Mahmoud Abu Teir, 17, from Um Touba, was taken prisoner on July 8 2014, after the soldiers stormed his family home shortly after midnight. He was then moved to al-Moskabiya, where he was stripped of his clothes, before he was cuffed, blindfolded, forced to kneel on the ground, and was kicked and beaten by the soldiers. He remained in al-Moskabiya, where he was subject to interrogation and torture, for 18 days. He repeatedly lost consciousness while under interrogation.[271]

---

268 Geneva Convention (IV), article 31.

269 Adalah to Attorney General: Shocking testimonies from Palestinian children who were tortured during arrest and interrogation, 4 June, 2014.

270 International Middle East Media Center, Child Detainees Continue to Face Abuse and Torture, 17 October, 2014.

271 Id.

3. Muhammad Hussein Rabee

Muhammad Hussein Rabee, 33, from Beit Anan village near Ramallah, suffered health complications as a result of tortured inflicted during his 40 days in al-Moskabiya. He was transferred to Hadassa Hospital and Shaare Zedek Medical Center for treatment. Rabee was detained on July 27 and his family did not find out his whereabouts until 30 days later. Rabee's lawyer said he had been "harshly tortured." Former prisoner Khaldun Jumhur, who was held in al-Moskabiya with Rabee, said that interrogators used a method involving pressure on the Rabee's neck and beat him on his hands, legs and head. A doctor at the detention center requested that Rabee undergo an X-ray, which was refused by the Shin Bet agency.[272]

E. Coercion

In addition to prohibiting torture, Article 31 of Geneva Convention (IV) provides that "no physical or moral coercion shall be exercised against protected persons, in particular to obtain information from them or from third parties."[273] Article 31 "covers all cases, whether the pressure is direct or indirect, obvious or hidden...coercion is forbidden for any purpose or motive whatever."[274]

The Israeli Security Agency (ISA), better known as the Shin Bet, particularly target Palestinian children because of their greater vulnerability. In 2004, Defense for Children International released a study on the recruitment of Palestinian children as collaborators. In the cases of recruitment of child collaborators studied by DCI, 24 children were beaten while under investigation, six were threatened with long sentences if they refused to collaborate, four were threatened with the demolition of their family homes, two were threatened with the arrest of family members, and one

---

272 Maan News Agency, Prisoner hospitalized after being tortured in Israeli jail, 3 September, 2014.

273 IV Geneva Convention, article 31.

274 IV Geneva Convention, article 31 Commentary.

child was threatened with sexual violence.[275] The ISA also offers rewards to would-be child collaborators. In the cases studied by DCI, 24 children were offered release, 11 children were offered sexual services; nine were offered money, four were offered work permits for themselves or family members, and eight children were offered more than one of these incentives.[276]

F. Home Invasions

The ISF's practice of raiding Palestinian homes, especially at night, in East Jerusalem violates the guarantees of privacy and the integrity of the home enshrined in conventional and customary IHL and IHRL. Its disparate application and enforcement of laws between Jewish-Israeli and Palestinian residents of oEJ violates the principle of nondiscrimination in the protection of human rights. Israel's failure to provide an effective remedy for these violations constitutes a further violation of its IHRL obligations.

1. Protection of the Home and Family Life

International humanitarian law and human rights treaties enshrine special protection for privacy, and particularly protection of the home and family environment from arbitrary interference.

Article 27 of Geneva Convention (IV) requires the occupying power to respect the personal honour and family rights of the occupied population.[277] At the core of this provision is the guarantee that "the family dwelling and home are therefore protected" and "cannot be the object of arbitrary interference."[278]
ICCPR Article 17 provides that "no one shall be subjected to arbitrary or unlawful interference with his privacy, family, home or correspondence."[279]

---

275 Defense for Children International, Use of Chidren in the Occuppied Palestinian Territories July 2004

276 Id.

277 Geneva Convention (IV), article 27.

278 ICRC Official Commentary to Geneva Convention (IV), article 27.

279 ICCPR, article 17.

Article 16 CRC similarly provides that "no child shall be subjected to arbitrary or unlawful interference with his or her privacy, family, or correspondence, nor to unlawful attacks on his or her honour and reputation."[280] Additionally, the CRC provides that no child should be subject to "cruel, inhuman or degrading treatment or punishment"[281] and that children accused of crimes have "the right to be treated with dignity."[282] The freedom from arbitrary and unlawful interference within the home is a customary principle of IHRL as evidenced by Article 12 UDHR and the various regional conventions safeguarding the home and family.[283] Additionally, it is a customary principle of IHL as evidenced by Article 46 of the Hague Regulations.

For the past several years, the Israeli Security Forces have engaged in a constant campaign of home raids in the West Bank, including oEJ. These raids generally take place after midnight and before 5 a.m.[284] without showing any warrant and without prior notice, often on suspicion of stone throwing or participation in an illegal demonstration.[285] ISF personnel routinely destroy property during these arrest operations.[286]

While the threat of home invasions is always present, the Israeli Security Forces stepped up raids in East Jerusalem precipitously during the assault on Gaza. The Land Research Center in Jerusalem recorded 153 home invasions in East Jerusalem in 2014,[287] including 91 in the month of July.[288] While the homes of families in Silwan and the Old

280 CRC, article 16.

281 CRC Article 37

282 CRC Article 40

283 See, e.g., American Convention on Human Rights, article 11; Arab Charter on Human Rights, article 21; European Convention on Human Rights Art. 8; The ASEAN Human Rights Declaration Art. 21: African Charter on the Rights and Welfare of the Child, art. 21.

284 Middle East Children's Alliance, Equal laws, discriminatory practice: the plight of Jerusalem children.

285 ARIJ, The Monthly Report on the Israeli Violations of Palestinian Rights in the Occupied City of Jerusalem, August, 2014,page 10; Defense for Children International, The Situation facing Palestinian Children, August 2011.

286 HRC, Concluding observations on the fourth periodic report of Israel par. 13, ARIJ, The Monthly Report on the Israeli Violations of Palestinian Rights in the Occupied City of Jerusalem, August, 2014,page 10.

287 ARIJ, The Monthly Report on the Israeli Violations of Palestinian Rights in the Occupied City of Jerusalem, August, 2014,page 10.

288 ARIJ, The Monthly Report on the Israeli Violations of Palestinian Rights in the Occupied City of Jerusalem, July 2014.

City accounted for more than half of the raids, families in Palestinian neighborhoods throughout oEJ were impacted.[289]

Home raids are carried out with utter disregard for the privacy and well being of the Palestinian families. In the occupied West Bank, for example, soldiers conduct raids on the civilian population for practice, without informing the victims that it is a training exercise.[290] Security forces often carry out the practice raids at night "to make it as real as possible," while using "houses, streets, people like cardboard practice targets."[291] In East Jerusalem, the intimidation that results from home raids, arrests, and harassment has forced many Palestinians out.[292]

2. Home Invasions as Collective Punishment

Article 33 of Geneva Convention (IV) bars states from carrying out collective punishment against the occupied population. This prohibition not only includes punishments imposed under penal law, but "penalties of any kind inflicted on persons or entire groups of persons...for acts that these persons have not committed.". The ISF's practice of detaining an entire family within the home during a search or arrest operation for a single individual runs afoul of Article 34 of Geneva Convention (IV), which bars the taking of hostages.[293] The ICRC Commentary to Article 34 elaborates the applicability of this prohibition in the context of home invasions.

> The modern form [of hostage taking], with which this article is concerned, is the taking of hostages as a means of intimidating the population in order to weaken its spirit of resistance and to prevent breaches of law and sabotage in order to ensure the

289 ARIJ, The Monthly Report on the Israeli Violations of Palestinian Rights in the Occupied City of Jerusalem, August, 2014,page 10.

290 The Guardian, Palestinian villages subject to Israeli mock raids not told they are exercises, 12 November, 2013.

291 Id.

292 The Nation, Israel's Land Grab in East Jerusalem, 17 April, 2013; Defense for Children International, The Situation facing Palestinian Children, August 2011.

293 UNICEF, Children in Israeli Military Detention Observations and Recommendations, February, 2013, page 14, Al Haq, Israeli forces holding Palestinians captive during house Raids, 2 March, 2006, e.g. Electronic Intifada, Family held at gunpoint as Israel arrests another Palestinian rights defender, 22 September, 2014.

security of the Detaining Power.[294]

The ICRC Commentary clarifies that "the word 'hostages' must be understood in the widest possible sense."[295] The practice of holding people hostage is "based on contempt for the principle of individual responsibility for breaches of law."[296] In this sense, Article 34 supplements the prohibition against collective punishment found in "Article 33, which embodies the principle of individual responsibility and the prohibition of collective penalties and measures of reprisal"[297] Further, Article 147 defines the unlawful confinement of protected persons as a grave breach of the Conventions.[298]

During home raids, families of suspects are awoken and often forced out of the home in the middle of the night.[299] In other raids, families are confined to one room and held captive while security forces search the home.[300] The invasion of privacy, evacuation from the home, confinement, and being held hostage while security forces search the home is collective punishment.

In a clear case of guilt by association, Israeli security forces ransacked the Shuafat family home of Tariq Abu Khdeir within hours of his release from home arrest and return to the United States.[301] The US State Department acknowledged that "members of the Khdeir family appeared to be singled out for arrest by the Israeli authorities."[302]

During the home invasions, property is destroyed, and Palestinians are physically injured. During one mid-August raid in Silwan, ISF personnel

294 Geneva Convention (IV), art. 34, commentary.

295 Id.

296 Id.

297 Id.

298 Geneva Convention (IV), art. 137.

299 UNICEF, Children in Israeli Military Detention Observations and Recommendations, February, 2013, page 14, http://www.unicef.org/oPt/UNICEF_oPt_Children_in_Israeli_Military_Detention_Observations_and_Recommendations_-_6_March_2013.pdf.

300 Al Haq, Israeli forces holding Palestinians captive during house Raids, 2 March, 2006

301 Huffington Post, Photos Show Tariq Abu Khdeir's Family Home Ransacked By Israeli Police, 19 July, 2014.

302 International Middle East Media Center, Abu Khdeir Family "Singled Out" for Arrest by Israeli Authorities, 22 August, 2014.

struck the father of a suspect in the face and eyes.[303] 21-year old Haitham Atyeh Qweider, who suffers from a developmental disability and is mute, was beaten by security forces who did not believe he could not speak.[304]

In yet another home invasion, more than 30 ISF personnel raided the apartment of the Abu Dalu family, assaulting 20-year old Ammar Abu Dalu, 17-year old Abdulrahman Maher Abu Dalu, and 16-year old Majd Jamal Siam with batons and rifle butts.[305] The ISF threatened to shoot the youths' parents as they tried to intervene.

All told, the ISF conducted 153 home invasions in East Jerusalem in 2014, including 91 in the month of July.[306] Most of these raids were conducted in the middle of the night.[307] ISF personnel often wear ski masks, fail to identify themselves as police, and use excessive force in entering, securing, and searching the premises.[308]

3. Psychological Impact of Home Invasions

These night raids and home invasions are disruptive to Palestinian family life and are particularly traumatic for children. Many children struggle with symptoms of post-traumatic stress that are disruptive to their emotional and intellectual development. Additionally, mothers and fathers are negatively impacted by the disruption to family life, and the family structure is undermined by lack of security in the home.

In December 2010, 60 Israeli childcare experts, psychologists and social workers sent an open letter to the Israeli prime minister and attorney general "calling on the authorities to monitor more closely police interactions with minors suspected of stone throwing in East Jerusalem."[309]

---

303 Silwanic, The masked forces assault the sick young man Haitham Qweider after raiding and damaging his family's building, 19 August, 2014.

304 id.

305 http://silwanic.net/?p=51159

306 ARIJ, The Monthly Report on the Israeli Violations of Palestinian Rights in the Occupied City of Jerusalem, July, 2014

307 Maan News Agency, Jerusalem faces largest surge in arrests since 2nd Intifada, 27 August, 2014.

308 Id.

309 Haaretz, Childcare experts condemn police treatment of Palestinian stone-throwers, 1 December, 2010.

The letter observed that children and teenagers have reported being "dragged out of their beds in the middle of the night" and arrested by "undercover detectives and special forces."[310] The letter noted a growing trend of underage suspects suffering from symptoms of post-traumatic stress including nightmares, sleepwalking and bedwetting.[311]

According to a 2005 article in the Journal of Child Abuse and Neglect, among school age Palestinian children in the West Bank including East Jerusalem, 54.7% had experienced a traumatic event and 34.1% were diagnosed with PTSD[312] According to another study, home invasions and detention of children can cause "some children to become 'closed off' (socially withdrawn and isolated), others 'act out' (become disobedient and aggressive) in response to their detention."[313] According to this study, children exhibited "many symptoms which are strongly suggestive of psychological trauma, such as nightmares, bed wetting and worsening academic performance."[314]

Children are afforded greater human rights protection under international conventions because of their tender age and susceptibility to trauma. When these rights are infringed by blowing the hinges off a door in order to harass a family in the middle of the night in raids that resemble "military tactics of Israeli forces in the occupied West Bank...rather than urban law enforcement"[315] the impact on children is traumatic, as evidenced above.

According to the Women's Center for Legal Aid and Counseling (WCLAC), a Palestinian human rights NGO, these night raids also have a devastating effect on women, families and entire communities. Mothers interviewed by WCLAC showed signs of "insomnia, tension headaches, hyper-vigilance, irritability, agitation, and panic attacks in addition to other physical and psychological symptoms that adversely impact their capacity to parent effectively...."[316]

---

310 Defense for Children International, Letter from Childcare experts to Israeli Police, 24 November, 2010, Available at http://www.dci-palestine.org/sites/default/files/letter_by_israeli_professionals_on_silwan.pdf

311 Id.

312 Post-traumatic stress disorder among school age Palestinian children, Vivian Khamis, 2005.

313 id.

314 The Impact of Detaining Children in Silwan, a Stone's Throw Away from Despair, Misha Gray, 2012; see also Association for Civil Rights in Israel, Shadow Report on the Implimentaion of the ICCPR in East Jerusalem, August, 2014.

315 Reuters, ArabEast Jerusalem Seethes with Protests and Raids, 28 August, 2014.

316 id.

Fathers described feeling helpless and guilty at their inability to protect their children, with consequences for their relationships with their children.[317] One father talking about the impact of his inability to protect his children from home invasions observed:

> Something changed in his life; he used to have the image of his father as the protector... This image has broken down. He used to behave [well] with his father and obey orders but now he doesn't because he believes that 'you are not the protector, father'"[318]

Home invasions thus destroy the fabric of society of Palestinian communities in oEJ and carry far-reaching social consequences.[319]

VI. Israeli Restrictions on Cultural and Religious Practices, Specifically Relating to the Al-Aqsa Mosque Compound

A. Background

1. Religious Significance of Jerusalem's Old City and Al-Aqsa Mosque Compound

The Old City of Jerusalem, located entirely in occupied East Jerusalem, carries great significance for the three Abrahamic faiths. The Old City has four quarters: Christian, Muslim, Jewish, and Armenian; and houses holy sites of Christianity, Islam and Judaism.[320] The Christian Quarter houses the Church of the Holy Sepulchre, where Christians believe Jesus

---

317 The Impact of Detaining Children in Silwan, a Stone's Throw Away from Despair, Misha Gray, 2012

318 Id.

319 Women's Center for Legal Aid and Counseling, Letter to UNICEF Re: Impact of Night Raids on Women and Children, 6 November, 2013

320 Chernofsky, Erica. "What Makes Jerusalem so Holy?" BBC News. BBC, 30 Oct. 2014. Web. 05 Nov. 2014.

was crucified and resurrected. The Muslim Quarter contains the Al-Aqsa Mosque Compound, also known to Muslims as the Haram al-Sharif (Noble Sanctuary), which is the third holiest site in Islam. The Compound is known to Jews as the Temple Mount and is regarded as the site of the two Jewish Temples of the Bible; as such, it is the holiest site in Judaism.[321]

Muslims visit the Al-Aqsa Mosque Compound site throughout the year. However, during the Muslim holy month of Ramadan – which in 2014 fell between 29 June and 27July – hundreds of thousands of Muslims prayed at the Mosque each Friday.

The Western Wall is located at the base of the western side of the Compound. In Judaism, the wall is regarded as a partial remnant of the second Jewish Temple. Some right-wing Jewish groups advocate building a new Jewish Temple in the reputed location of the old Temple—where the Al-Aqsa Mosque and Dome of the Rock today stand.

2. The Legal Status of the Al-Aqsa Mosque Compound

The Al-Aqsa Mosque Compound remains under the custodianship of the King of Jordan and the administration of the Jordanian Islamic Waqf in Jerusalem. This understanding was acknowledged by Israel in the Washington Declaration, which formally ended the state of war between Israel and Jordan, and the 1994 Israeli-Jordan Peace Treaty.[322] In March 2013, King Abdullah II of Jordan and President Mahmoud Abbas of Palestine executed an agreement that reaffirmed Palestinian sovereignty over East Jerusalem and the King's custodianship of the Jerusalem Holy Places, including the Mosque Compound.[323]

---

321 The term "Al-Aqsa Mosque Compound" is used consistently throughout this section.

322 Wither Jerusalem?: Proposals and Positions Concerning the Future of Jerusalem. Moshe Hirsh, Deborah Housen-Couriel and Ruth Lapidoth. Martinus Nijhoff Publishers. Kluwer Law International, 1995. For an English-language text of the Washington Declaration, see, "The Washington Declaration" on the King Hussein Library, at http://www.kinghussein.gov.jo/w-declaration.html. For an English-language text of the 1994 Jordan-Israel Peace Treaty, see http://www.kinghussein.gov.jo/peacetreaty.html.

323 Agreement between King Abdullah II Bin al-Hussein, the Custodian of the Holy Sites in Jerusalem, and Dr. Mahmoud Abbas, President of the State of Palestine, Head of Palestinian Liberation Organization, and President of the Palestinian National Authority (March 31, 2013), English translation available at http://kingabdullah.jo/index.php/en_US/news/view/id/10779/videoDisplay/1.html.

3. History of Nationalist Violence Against Palestinians at the Al-Aqsa Mosque Compound

As a sacred site to the global Muslim community and a symbol of Palestinian national aspirations, the Al-Aqsa Mosque Compound has, since 1967, been a target of nationalist violence by Israeli extremists and Israeli politicians seeking to brandish their right-wing credentials through confrontation with the Palestinian population. Among these incidents:

- In August 1969, an Australian Christian-Zionist, Denis Rohan, burnt the pulpit of Al-Aqsa Mosque.

- On April 11, 1982, an American-born Israeli, Alan Goodman, fired an automatic weapon at Muslim worshippers at the Compound, killing two and wounding eleven.

- In January 1984, members of the "Jewish Underground" terrorist organization were arrested for plotting to blow up multiple shrines on the Compound.

- On October 8, 1990, the ISF killed 21 Palestinians and injured over 150 others following clashes triggered by the visit of Jewish settlers to the Compound.

- On September 23, 1996, the Israeli government opened an entrance to a large, ancient tunnel near the Compound. 70 Palestinians and 17 Israeli soldiers were killed in the ensuing demonstrations.

- Ariel Sharon's visit to the Compound, accompanied by over 1,000 police officers, on September 28, 2000 sparked the Al-Aqsa (Second) Intifada.[324]

---

324 Hatuqa, Dalia et el. "Timeline: Al-Aqsa Mosque" Al Jazeera. Al Jazeera. 30 Oct 2014. Web. 25 Nov 2014.

4. Jewish Access to the Compound and Violations of the Compound's Sanctity

The Chief Rabbinate of Israel prohibits Jews from entering or praying at the Compound because of the site's holiness. Israel's two Chief Rabbis jointly reiterated this ban in December 2013. The Chief Sephardic Rabbi, Yitzhak Yosef, on 7 November 2014 condemned the "B-rate rabbis" who encourage Jews to pray at the site for "adding fuel to the fire."[325] Nevertheless, the Supreme Court of Israel has recognized the right of individual Jews to pray at the Temple Mount under a 1967 Israeli law that guarantees freedom of access for all faiths to their holy places.[326] However, the Supreme Court has recognized that this right can be restricted through time, place and manner restrictions, such as a ban on demonstrative prayer or prayer involving religious paraphernalia.[327] The ISF have historically maintained such in the interest of maintaining public order and the Israeli Supreme Court has generally upheld them.[328]

In recent years, a growing number of Jewish Israelis from the national-religious movement have flouted the Israeli rabbinical establishment by visiting the Al-Aqsa Mosque Compound under heavily-armed ISF escort.[329] Elements of this movement, most notably the Temple Mount Faithful group, openly seek to replace the Muslim Holy Places at the Compound with a "Third Temple." The increase in the number and visibility of visits to the Compound by members of this extremist element, including Israeli MPs, and the corresponding discussion of destroying the Muslim Holy Places have outraged Muslims worldwide and Palestinians of all faiths.

Visits by extremist Jewish-Israelis from the national-religious movement to the al-Aqsa Mosque Compound increased over the relevant period. In the

---

325 Yair Ettinger, "Jews forbidden from going to Temple Mount, says chief Sephardi rabbi," Haaretz, Nov. 7, 2014, http://www.haaretz.com/news/national/1.625233.

326 Protection of the Holy Places Law 1967, art. 1. This guarantee of freedom of access to the Holy Places was constitutionalized in 1980 as Article 3 of the Basic Law: Jerusalem.

327 See generally Shmuel Berkovitz, The Temple Mount and the Western Wall in Israeli Law (Jerusalem Institute for Israel Studies, 2001) 80-83.

328 Id.

329 The national-religious movement, also called "Religious Zionism," is an ideology that combines Zionism and Judaism. It recasts Zionism, originally a political movement initiated by secular Jews, as an expression of divine will and a religious obligation. Most adherents of the national-religious movement embrace right-wing politics and are represented in the Israeli Knesset by the Likud, Jewish Home, and smaller far-right parties.

circumstances just discussed, these visits were inherently provocative, were accompanied by a massive ISF presence, and severely curtailed the freedom of access and worship for Palestinians.

During the summer of 2014, Jewish Israelis were allowed to enter the Al-Aqsa Mosque Compound on all days, except Friday and Saturday, between 7:00am and 11:00am, under police escort and protection. During these times, Muslim worshippers were denied access to the Mosque.[330] During the week of August 12, the ISF arrested two Palestinians, including one woman, for protesting these restrictions on Palestinian access and worship.[331]

5. Ibrahimi Mosque in Hebron as the Model of Partition

Israeli restrictions and provocations at the Al-Aqsa Mosque Compound during the relevant period should be understood in the context of the provocateurs' ultimate goal of marginalizing or even eliminating Al-Aqsa's status as a Muslim religious site and Palestinian national symbol by establishing a permanent Jewish-Israeli presence there. Many Palestinians believe that the ultimate goal of these provocations is the physical division of Al-Aqsa Mosque Compound between Muslims and Jews, as has occurred at the Ibrahimi Mosque in Hebron.[332]

There is increasing popular and institutional support for the right-wing national-religious Jewish organizations that seek to alter the delicate status quo at the Compound.

Israeli public officials have expressed their support for the goals of these movements. On 25 February 2014, Likud MP and deputy Knesset speaker Moshe Feiglin convened a Knesset debate on "the loss of Israeli

330 The Monthly Report on the Israeli Violations of Palestinian Rights in the Occupied City of Jerusalem June 2014. Rep. Jerusalem: Arab Studies Society – Land Research Center (LRC), 2014. Print.

331 Protection of Civilians Weekly Report, August 12-18. Tech. Occupied Palestinian Territory: United Nations Office for the Coordination of Humanitarian Affairs, 2014. United Nations Office for the Coordination of Humanitarian Affairs. Web. 12 Nov. 2014.

332 Middle East Monitor. "Saleh: We Will Not Surrender in Face of Israeli Violations against Al-Aqsa". 11 Nov 2014. Web. 25 Nov 2014.

sovereignty over the Temple Mount."[333] Feiglin has urged the Israeli government to exercise "sovereignty" over the Compound by, among other things, allowing Israeli nationals to unfurl Israeli flags at the site.[334] In the course of that debate, Israeli lawmakers discussed revoking the Waqf's administration of the Compound. Another Likud MP, Miri Regev, backs Feiglin's initiative and has stated, "[w]e will reach a situation where the Temple Mount will be like the Cave of the Patriarchs [Ibrahimi Mosque], days for Jews and days for Muslims."[335]

Palestinian concerns over the possible partition of the Al-Aqsa Mosque Compound are based largely on the precedent of the Ibrahimi Mosque in Hebron, known to Jews as the Tomb of the Patriarchs. After Hebron and the Ibrahimi Mosque came under Israeli control in 1967, Jewish settlers began colonizing areas surrounding the Mosque with Israeli government support. Exploiting the heavy ISF presence around the settlements and the Mosque, these settlers began entering the Mosque to pray. In 1994, Baruch Goldstein, an American-born Israeli settler living in the Hebron settlement of Kiryat Arba, entered the Mosque in his army uniform and massacred 29 Palestinian worshippers. In the protests that ensued, another 25 Palestinians and 5 Israelis were killed.

The Israeli government used the massacre to consolidate its hold on Hebron and the Ibrahimi Mosque. It imposed a two-week curfew on Palestinian residents of Hebron, closed over 500 businesses on Shuhada Street, the main commercial road leading to the Mosque, and kept the Mosque closed for nine months. When it reopened, the Mosque had been partitioned, with separate areas for Muslim and Jewish worshippers. The partition, the closure of Shuhada Street, and the additional restrictions

---

333 Ben Lynfield, "Mounting tension: Israel's Knesset debates proposal to enforce its sovereignty at Al-Aqsa Mosque - a move seen as 'an extreme provocation to Muslims worldwide," The Independent, 26 Feb. 2014, http://www.independent.co.uk/news/world/middle-east/mounting-tension-israels-knesset-debates-proposal-to-enforce-its-sovereignty-at-alaqsa-mosque--a-move-seen-as-an-extreme-provocation-to-muslims-worldwide-9155575.html.

334 Baroud, Ramzy. "Saving Al-Aqsa Mosque." Al Jazeera. Al Jazeera, 6 Mar. 2014. Web. 12 Nov. 2014.

335 Ben Lynfield, "Mounting tension: Israel's Knesset debates proposal to enforce its sovereignty at Al-Aqsa Mosque - a move seen as 'an extreme provocation to Muslims worldwide,'" The Independent, Feb. 26, 2014, http://www.independent.co.uk/news/world/middle-east/mounting-tension-israels-knesset-debates-proposal-to-enforce-its-sovereignty-at-alaqsa-mosque--a-move-seen-as-an-extreme-provocation-to-muslims-worldwide-9155575.html. Some Israeli leaders, such as Housing Minister Uri Ariel, have gone even further by proclaiming that Al-Aqsa Mosque will ultimately be destroyed and replaced by a new Jewish Temple. Moore, Jack. "Israel: Al-Aqsa Mosque 'Will be Replaced by Jewish Temple' Claims Housing Minister Uri Ariel". International Business Times. 04 Nov 2014. Web. 25 Nov 2014.

on movement for Palestinians in Hebron that were imposed after the massacre remain in effect today.

Against this history, Palestinians fear that the efforts of the Jewish national-religious movement to alter the status quo at the Al-Aqsa Compound, with the protection and support of the ISF, as the first stage of an operational plan to partition or even take over the Compound.[336]

6. Settlement Enclaves In and Around the Old City

Palestinian concerns that Israel is "Hebronizing" East Jerusalem are further supported by mounting Israeli efforts to establish "settlement enclaves" within Palestinian neighborhoods in and around the Old City.[337] Nearly 2,000 Israeli settlers live in the heart of Palestinian neighborhoods in and around the Old City, including the Muslim and Christian Quarters, Silwan, Ras al-'Amud, a-Tur, Abu Dis, and Sheikh Jarrah.[338] According to B'Tselem, an Israeli human rights NGO, these settler groups seek control the main roads leading to the Al-Aqsa Mosque Compound as a means of controlling the Compound itself.[339] While these settlement enclaves are initiated by private settler organizations, Israel support this initiative by using the ISF to effect the takeover of Palestinian properties and protect their Jewish settlers and by transferring government assets into the control of these settler organizations.

These settlement enclaves not only violate Article 49(6) of Geneva Convention (IV), which prohibits an occupying power from transferring its civilian population into occupied territory, but also infringe upon the freedom of movement, privacy and security of the protected Palestinian population. These enclaves undermine the character of Palestinian neighborhoods in East Jerusalem in that they invariably lead to restrictions on the use

---

336 Ir Amin. 2013. "Dangerous Liaison: The Dynamics of the Rise of the Temple Movements and their Implications". Web. Available at:<http://www.altro.co.il/uploads/org_252/File/Dangerous%20Liaison.pdf>

337 Cook, Jonathan. "Israel Tightens Grip Around al-Aqsa Mosque". Al Jazeera. 23 April 2014. Web. 24 Nov 2014.

338 United Nations Office for the Coordination of Humanitarian Affairs Occupied Palestinian Territory. 2012. "Settlement in Palestinian Residential Areas in East Jerusalem." Web. 24 Nov 2014.

339 B'Tselem. "Settler Enclaves in East Jerusalem". 1 Jan 2011. Web. 25 Nov 2014.

of the surrounding public space and constrain the growth of Palestinian residential areas. ISF personnel stationed at these enclaves understand their mission as protecting the settlers, even when those settlers attack their Palestinian neighbors, rather than upholding the law. Thus, the ISF presence around the enclaves raise tensions and undermines the security of Palestinian residents, often forcing them to move elsewhere. [340] The settlement enclaves thus constitute a major trigger of forcible transfer of Palestinians in East Jerusalem.

B. IHL and IHRL Violations Relating to Freedom of Movement

1. Restrictions on Palestinian Access to East Jerusalem: Israel's Separation Policy and Permit Regime

Palestinians from other parts of the West Bank and from the Gaza Strip are prohibited from entering East Jerusalem without a permit from the Israeli military authorities. This permit regime is part of a policy of separating East Jerusalem from other parts of the West Bank; and the West Bank, including East Jerusalem, from the Gaza Strip.[341] These policies and practices of separation started in the early 1990s and have progressively expanded. Following the outbreak of the Second Intifada, Israel imposed a comprehensive closure system on Palestinians within the oPt. For the West Bank, this system included physical obstacles (e.g. checkpoints, roadblocks, the Wall) and administrative restrictions (e.g. prohibited roads, permit requirements, age restrictions).[342] These measures "physically reinforce [Israel's] control" over East Jerusalem and attempt to "completely sever it from the West Bank."[343]

---

340 United Nations Office for the Coordination of Humanitarian Affairs Occupied Palestinian Territory. 2012. "Settlement in Palestinian Residential Areas in East Jerusalem." Web. 24 Nov 2014.

341 Act Palestine Forum. 2013."The 'Permit Regime' and Israeli Attacks of Palestinian Freedom of Worship". Web. 24 Nov 2014.

342 United Nations Office for the Coordination of Humanitarian Affairs Occupied Palestinian Territory. 2012. "West Bank Movement and Access Update". Web. 24 Nov 2014.

343 Al-Haq, "The Jerusalem Trap", (2010), 18.

Gaza's separation from East Jerusalem is far more comprehensive. Throughout the relevant period, Israel continued to restrict movement of Palestinians between Gaza, Israel and the West Bank, including East Jerusalem, to "exceptional humanitarian cases, with an emphasis on urgent medical cases." [344] During 2014, less than 7,000 Palestinians entered Israel from Gaza per month through the Erez crossing, mostly businesspeople, medical patients and their companions.[345]

As a result, approximately four million Palestinians in the oPt are prohibited from entering East Jerusalem without Israeli-issued permits.[346] The bureaucratic procedure for Palestinians to obtain permits through the Israeli Civil Administration (ICA) is complicated, long and often humiliating. Palestinians in the oPt must obtain a magnetic-card ID after the age of 16 before applying. As part of this process, Palestinians must have their hands electronically scanned. The ICA has over 100 types of permits that governs the movement of Palestinians, including permits for worshipers attending Friday prayers at Al-Aqsa Mosque and clerics working at the Mosque.[347]

The permit system is enforced through a network of checkpoints along the route of the Wall. As of February 2014, Israel maintained 99 fixed checkpoints in the West Bank. Access to East Jerusalem is strictly controlled by 16 checkpoints. Palestinians who are able to obtain permits may only use four of these checkpoints to enter East Jerusalem. The vast majority of permits issued during Ramadan for access to Al-Aqsa Mosque require Palestinians to enter East Jerusalem through the congested Qalandiya checkpoint, south of Ramallah.

Israel's movement and access restrictions within the oPt, including East Jerusalem, violate the fundamental right of the Palestinian population to freedom of movement. As an occupying power, Israel is obligated under Article 27 of Geneva Convention (IV) to respect the fundamental rights of the protected Palestinian population, including the right to move freely.

---

344 See generally Gisha, "Gaza Access and Movement: 2014 Summary," Jan. 20, 2015, http://gisha.org/en-blog/2015/01/20/gaza-access-and-movement-2014-summary-2/.

345 Id.

346 Id.

347 Chaim Levinson, "Israel has 101 different types of permits governing Palestinian movement," Haaretz, Dec. 23, 2011, http://www.haaretz.com/print-edition/news/israel-has-101-different-types-of-permits-governing-palestinian-movement-1.403039

While freedom of movement is subject to restrictions based on military necessity, it cannot be "suspended in a general manner"; rather, "the regulations concerning occupation...are based on the idea of the personal freedom of civilians remaining in general unimpaired."[348] Additionally, Article 32 of the Convention prohibits the occupying army from causing physical suffering to protected persons, including "any measures of brutality," while Article 33(1) prohibits "any measures of intimidation or of terrorism" by the occupying power against the occupied population.

Moreover, Article 13 of the UDHR and Article 12 of the ICCPR give everyone who is lawfully present within a state the right to "liberty of movement" within the borders of that state. Thus, state authorities may not restrict the entry or stay of lawfully-present persons to a defined part of its territory.[349] Freedom of movement is an indispensable condition for the enjoyment of other rights, including the right to work, an adequate standard of living, health, education and the protection of family life. Freedom of movement cannot be restricted except in situations that "are provided by law, are necessary to protect national security, public order, public health or morals or the rights and freedoms of others, and are consistent with the other rights recognized" in the ICCPR.[350] Any limitation upon the freedom of movement must be necessary, proportional and may not nullify the principle of liberty of movement.[351]

Israel's restrictions on Palestinian access to East Jerusalem violates these rights insofar as accessing East Jerusalem from other parts of the oPt constitutes movement within the occupied territory, rather than entry into the State of Israel. Unlike the vast majority of Palestinians living in the oPt, Jewish settlers and tourists may move freely between oEJ and other parts of the West Bank, and between the West Bank and Israel, without permits.[352] Because the permit regime rests on distinctions based on national identity – an identity that is based on race and/or national origin and forms the basis for Israel's citizenship laws[353] – it violates Israel's obligation to uphold

---

348 Pictet J (Ed), Commentary to Geneva Convention IV relative to the protection of civilian persons in time of war (ICRC: Geneva: 1958), 202.

349 Id.

350 ICCPR Article 12(3).

351 Human Rights Committee CCPR General Comment No. 27: Article 12 (Freedom of Movement)

352 B'tselem, "Background on the Restriction of Movement". 1 Jan 2011. Web. 24 Nov 2014.

its IHL and IHRL obligations in the oPt without discrimination.[354]

2. Restrictions on Access to East Jerusalem during Ramadan

During Ramadan, Muslims participate in nightly prayers at Al-Aqsa Mosque in additional to the regular Friday mid-day prayers. While Israel generally eases permit restrictions during Ramadan, it applied stricter standards during Ramadan in 2014, severely limiting the number of Palestinians allowed to enter the Mosque Compound.[355] On the first Friday of Ramadan, July 4th, only 11,000 Palestinians with West Bank IDs were allowed to enter East Jerusalem, a 90 percent decline from the first Friday in Ramadan the previous year.[356]

Israel raised age-based restrictions on entry to East Jerusalem. During Ramadan 2014, only Palestinian men over 50 and women over 40 with West Bank IDs were allowed to enter East Jerusalem without permits. These restrictions were significantly more restrictive than those for Ramadan 2013, when men above 40, boys below 12 and women of all ages were allowed entry to East Jerusalem without permits.[357] In 2014, men under age 45 were banned from crossing the checkpoints into East Jerusalem on Fridays throughout Ramadan for fear that they would visit Al-Aqsa Mosque.[358] This restriction applied even to East Jerusalem residents

---

353 See Dugard and Reynolds, Apartheid, International Law, and the Occupied Palestinian Territory, supra n. 6, at 885-891 (concluding that "Jews and Palestinians are constructed and perceived both by themselves and by external actors as stable and permanent groups distinct from each other, and therefore can be considered as different racial groups for the purposes of the definition of apartheid").

354 See generally Alon Margalit and Sarah Hibbin, "Unlawful Presence of Protected Persons in Occupied Territory? An Analysis of Israel's Permit Regime and Expulsions from the West Bank under the Law of Occupation," 13 Yearbook of International Humanitarian Law 245 (2011).

355 For example, during Ramadan 2013, Israel allowed Palestinians over age 60 to enter East Jerusalem and Israel without a permit throughout the month, while it allowed women of all ages and men over 40 were able to enter for Friday prayers without a permit. Israel claims that over 1 million entries by oPt Palestinians into East Jerusalem and Israel during Ramadan 2013. See http://www.israelemb.org/washington/NewsAndEvents/Pages/Over-a-million-Palestinians-entered-Israel-during-month-of-Ramadan-2013.aspx.

356 UN OCHA Protection of Civilians Weekly Report, 1-7 June 2014, http://www.ochaopt.org/documents/ocha_opt_protection_of_civilians_weekly_report_2014_7_11_english.pdf.

357 Protection of Civilians Weekly Report, July 1-7. Tech. Occupied Palestinian Territory: United Nations Office for the Coordination of Humanitarian Affairs, 2014. United Nations Office for the Coordination of Humanitarian Affairs. Web. 12 Nov. 2014.

358 Response by Ir Amin to Fourth Periodic Report of Israel, September 2014.

holding Israeli permanent residency (Jerusalem IDs) and irrespective of whether they were visiting the Mosque.

Table 1

Palestinians Allowed to Enter Occupied East Jerusalem during Ramadan 2014 compared to Ramadan 2013[359]

	Ramadan 2013	Ramadan 2014	% of 2013 number
1st Friday	200-250,000	July 4 -11,000	4.4 – 5.5 %
2nd Friday	137,550	July 11 - 9,990	7.3%
3rd Friday	114,416	July 18- 16,301	14.2%
4th Friday	104,500	July 25- 8,000	7.7%
Laylat-ul-Qadr	400,000	July 24- ~ 5,000	~ 1.25 %
Total	956,466 – 1,006,466	50,291	5-5.26 %

3. Restrictions on Palestinians in the Hebron District: Collective Punishment

Three Israeli nationals disappeared in the southern West Bank on June 12, 2014, in a suspected kidnapping. Effective June 13, 2014, the Israeli authorities invalidated the permits of Hebron District residents to access oEJ and Israel. Furthermore, Palestinian men from the Hebron District between the ages of 16 and 50 were forbidden from crossing the Wadi al-Nar checkpoint into the central and southern West Bank, effectively confining them to the southern West Bank and impacting their ability to earn a living or visit family.[360] These restriction continued through the first two weeks of Ramadan.[361] On 7 July, Israel lifted most movement restrictions on Palestinian residents of the Hebron District.

359 UN OCHA Reports

360 Protection of Civilians Weekly Report, June 17-23. Tech. Occupied Palestinian Territory: United Nations Office for the Coordination of Humanitarian Affairs, 2014. United Nations Office for the Coordination of Humanitarian Affairs. Web. 12 Nov. 2014.

361 Ibid.

The collective punishment of protected population is forbidden under Article 50 of the Hague Regulations and Article 33 of Geneva Convention (IV), which prohibit an occupying power from using "collective penalties and likewise measures of intimidation." Israel's closure of the Hebron District plainly constitutes collective punishment insofar as the whole of the District's 700,000 residents were punished for acts for which they bear no responsibility. It is an extension of Israel's "Dahiya doctrine" of causing suffering among civilians for political rather than military objectives and with punitive intent.[362] These policies and practices of collective punishment constitute war crimes under Article 147 of Geneva Convention (IV).

C. IHL and IHRL Violations Relating to the Al-Aqsa Mosque Compound

1. Restrictions on Palestinian Access to the Mosque Compound

Tighter restrictions on Palestinian access to the Al-Aqsa Mosque Compound mirrored those on access to East Jerusalem. On July 4, the first Friday of Ramadan, all worshippers under 50 years of age – men and women – were banned from entering the mosque.[363] Furthermore, many Palestinian worshippers over age 50 were arbitrarily denied access to the Mosque.

Um Sa'ed, 68 years old, who had worked at Al-Aqsa Mosque since January 2014, was banned from entering the Mosque. She testified:

> We have been suffering from the Israeli forces…They start taking our IDs, they start preventing us from entering, making us wait for a long time, and not allowing us to wait at the gates, they force us to leave. The settlers go and come as they like and we are not allowed to go… They used to keep us till 2 or 3 pm outside, preventing us from entering, and if we start screaming allahu

362 For more information on Israel's "Dahiya doctrine," see Report of the United Nations Fact-Finding Mission on the Gaza Conflict, A/HRC/12/48 (Sept. 25, 2009), paras. 62. 1194-1216.

363 Ma'an News Agency. "Israel Imposes Ramadan Restrictions on Aqsa". 04 July 2014. Web. 10 Dec 2014.

> akbar, they take our photos, take us to the police station, and prevent some of us to enter Aqsa for 2 weeks... or 40 days. ... When they saw us trying to prevent the settlers from getting in, they started using gas bombs, napalm that burns the material of the clothes. Many people were really burned, because of using these kinds of bombs. So they used to push us and harass us, because you know as a woman culturally they shouldn't touch us, but they used to come to try and push us, in order to force us to leave. And many people were really harassed, beaten as well. ... We are victims of Israeli police harassment. Sometimes we have to pray outside the mosque, in the streets, because they don't allow us to get in.[364]

These restrictions continued throughout Ramadan and beyond, triggering protests and a heavy-handed ISF response. On 30 October 2014, the Israeli authorities forced the first complete closure of the Mosque Compound since 1967 after right-wing Jewish groups urged supporters to march on the Compound to protest the shooting of a right-wing Jewish activist, Yehuda Glick, in West Jerusalem.[365] Glick was attacked at a conference of Israeli right-wing groups pressing to revoke the status quo at the Compound, increase Jewish access, and ultimately establish a new Jewish Temple on the site.[366] The Mosque Compound was reopened on 31 October, with nearly 3,000 ISF personnel deployed in the Old City and its surroundings.[367] Israeli authorities barred men under age 50 from entering the Compound.[368]

2. ISF Crowd Control Measures at the Mosque Compound

ISF personnel regularly use violent means to disperse worshippers at Al-Aqsa Mosque as soon as prayers end. These techniques include tear gas, sound bombs, rubber-coated bullets, sewage or "skunk water,"

---

364 Interview by CCPRJ Fieldworker, 19 October 2014

365 Baker, "Clashes Erupt as Israeli Police Kill Palestinian."

366 Lewis, Renee. "Israel Bars Palestinians Under 50 from Entering Al-Aqsa Mosque". Al Jazeera. 31 Oct 2014. Web. 25 Nov 2014

367 Baker, Luke. "Muslim Men Over 50 Pray at Jerusalem's Aqsa Mosque Amid Security," Reuters, 31 Oct. 2013.

368 Id.

and rifle-butt strikes.[369] These techniques are also employed against Palestinians who are denied entry to Al-Aqsa (generally men under 50 who are authorized to cross the checkpoints into East Jerusalem with their commercial or work permits) and take to praying in the nearby streets.[370]

On October 8, 2014, Samah, who works inside the library of Al-Aqsa Mosque, was severely beaten by ISF personnel just outside the Mosque Compound.

> I arrived to my work, I noticed that there were checkpoints in the streets, nobody was allowed to enter. So instead of going to the checkpoint to ask, because I saw the same soldier who beat me last time, I decided to go to another gate...so I walked towards one of the guards and I was standing speaking with them, and they told me it wasn't allowed even for the workers to enter Aqsa. So I didn't go to the policemen, didn't make any argument with them or anything. I was just standing, talking with one of the guards. I noticed two Russian Israeli police pointing at me. And one of them [was] the one that beat me last time...the same woman with other soldiers...

Her colleagues – other women who worked in Al-Aqsa and who were also denied entry at the gates of the Mosque Compound – attempted to protect Samah by encircling her. She then advised a nearby police officer that the officer who beat her last time was approaching:

> I said to the police officer, she's coming to beat me, I didn't do anything, and you need to protect me. But instead of doing anything he started shouting at me. And immediately she started attacking me. She pushed me from my body, and the other Russian guy, beat me in my legs, so I fell down. When I fell down, she sat on my chest and took my headdress and covered my face so I couldn't see anything. And she started strangling me with both hands. I wasn't able to breathe. I tried to breathe, so another one of the soldiers took my hands and handcuffed me in a bad way. The blood started going from my hands. They were beating me all over my body and I was not able to see.

369 The Monthly Report on the Israeli Violations of Palestinian Rights in the Occupied City of Jerusalem July 2014. Rep. Jerusalem: Arab Studies Society – Land Research Center (LRC), 2014.

370 Protection of Civilians Weekly Report, July 1-7. Tech. Occupied Palestinian Territory: United Nations Office for the Coordination of Humanitarian Affairs, 2014. United Nations Office for the Coordination of Humanitarian Affairs. Web. 12 Nov. 2014.

> They started grabbing me from my legs while my hands were cuffed and I couldn't see ... after 8 meters from beating me I felt in that moment that I lost all of my clothes. They stood me up after 8 meters and that woman took off my hijab and threw it on the ground in a very humiliating way. And she grabbed me by my hair and started beating me with her knees in my back while the other soldier took me by the hands even though my hands are cuffed and started beating me in the side. They pulled me by my hair in this way for almost a half kilometer while my hands are cuffed, bleeding, and they are beating me and started calling me bad names... "whore, this is the land of Israel, go to Gaza..." all the time. .. and of course they closed the roads, so people weren't able to come and help me. I was in my neighborhood, the neighborhood I grew up in [in the old city], so I started calling my friends, family, especially my father, because I was thinking at least if he hears my voice someone will know that they're taking me to jail.

As discussed in section IV, supra, the unjustified or excessive use of force by ISF in East Jerusalem, including the Al-Aqsa Mosque Compound, implicate many of Israel's obligations under international humanitarian law, including humane treatment, protection of life and property, and the prohibition on collective punishment. These practices also violate the rights of the Palestinian population under international human rights law, including the freedoms of assembly and expression, rights to family and cultural life, and the protection of cultural property.

3. Failure to Recognize and Protect Non-Jewish Holy Sites

The aforementioned IHL and IHRL violations at the Al-Aqsa Mosque Compound during the relevant period reflects a culture of impunity for infringements on the rights of access and worship for non-Jews. This culture of impunity is fostered by Israel's longstanding and systematic failure to protect the integrity of non-Jewish holy sites in occupied East Jerusalem.

Israel's Protection of Holy Places Law 1967 provides that "[t]he Holy Places shall be protected from desecration and any other violation and from anything likely to violate the freedom of access of the members of the different religions to the places sacred to them or their feelings with regard to those places."[371] Notwithstanding this law, the U.S. State Department, in its 2009 Report on International Religious Freedom, has observed that:

> The Government [of Israel] implements regulations only for Jewish sites. Non-Jewish Holy Sites do not enjoy legal protection... because the Government does not recognize them as official holy sites... while well-known sites have de facto protection as a result of their international importance, many Muslim and Christian sites are neglected, inaccessible, or threatened by property developers and municipalities.[372]

These restrictions on Palestinian access to East Jerusalem and its Holy Sites violate Israel's obligation to uphold the free exercise of religion, which is enshrined in IHL, conventional IHRL including the ICCPR, and customary international law. Article 27 of Geneva Convention (IV) guarantees that protected persons are entitled in all circumstances to respect for their religious convictions and practices, including the integrity of their religious sites. Furthermore, Article 18 ICCPR, which protects the "freedom to have or to adopt a religion or belief of his choice, and freedom, either individually or in community with others and in public or private, to manifest his religion or belief in worship, observance, practice and teaching," embodies an obligation on State parties to preserve the integrity of worship sites of all faiths.

VII. Israeli Settlement Enterprise in Occupied East Jerusalem

A. Settlement Activity During the Relevant Period

It is now beyond doubt that Israel's settlement enterprise in the oPt violates Article 49(6) of Geneva Convention (IV), which prohibits the occupying power from transferring, directly or indirectly, its civilian population into the territory it occupies[373]; constitutes a grave breach of

---

371 Protection of Holy Places Law, June 27, 1967, SH 499, 75

372 2 US State Department, Bureau of Democracy, Human Rights and Labor, International Religious Freedom Report, 2009: Israel and the occupied territories (October 26, 2009).

373 Legal Consequences of a Wall, supra n. 2, at ¶ 120.

international humanitarian law[374]; is an internationally-wrongful act insofar as it severely impedes the exercise by the Palestinian people of its right to self-determination; and constitutes a war crime.[375]

During the relevant period, Israel announced five major settlement expansions in occupied East Jerusalem or in "greater Jerusalem," thereby further compromising oEJ's link with the rest of the oPt. These announcements furthered Israel's longstanding goal of territorial and demographic domination of Jerusalem. This goal of Jewish-Israeli dominion over Jerusalem drives the expropriation of Palestinian land and forced transfers of the Palestinian population to make way for additional Jewish settlements in East Jerusalem, the pace of which has accelerated in recent years. From 2000 to 2012, the number of settlement housing units in occupied East Jerusalem increased from 41,324 to 54,216, bringing a twenty-percent increase in the Jewish population. A further 6,431 units were approved in 2012 alone.[376]

Between June and September of 2014, Israel announced or advanced a number of settlement units, national parks, and transportation infrastructure in oEJ, fueling the unrest and adding to the IHL and IHRL violations documented throughout this submission.

1. Settlements

- On 6 June 2014, Israel issued construction tenders for 400 housing units in the Ramat Shlomo settlement, to be built on land belonging to Palestinian neighborhood of Shuafat (a distinct Jerusalem village prior to Israel's expansion of municipal Jerusalem in 1967). On 12 September 2014, an additional 31 units were added to this tender.[377]

- On 4 July 2014, Israel announced the construction of 243 housing

---

374 Protocol Additional to the Geneva Conventions of 12 August 1949, and relating to the Protection of Victims of International Armed Conflicts (Protocol I), 8 June 1977, art. 85(4)(a).

375 Rome Statute of the International Criminal Court, art. 8(2)(b)(viii).

376 "Response by Ir Amin to the Fourth Periodic Report of Israel (CCPR/C/ISR/4)," pg. 16. Ir Amin. September 2014.

377 al Sanara, 6 June 2014.

units in the Pisgat Zeev and Har Homa settlements.[378]

- On 25 August 2014, Israel issued construction tenders for 708 residential units in Gilo settlement.[379]

- On 24 September 2014, a previously announced plan for a new settlement, Givat Hamatos, was expanded from 2355 housing units to 2561 units. The new settlement will be built on land confiscated from the Palestinian neighborhood of Beit Safafa in oEJ and the town of Beit Jala, in the Bethlehem District.[380]

Also during the relevant period, Jewish settlers, backed by ISF, continued to establish settlement enclaves in Palestinian neighborhoods surrounding the Old City. In the Palestinian neighborhood of Silwan, dozens of Israeli settlers moved in overnight under ISF protection on October 19, 2014.[381] This takeover, which followed a similar influx of settlers in late September, doubled the number of Jewish settlers in Silwan.[382] Currently, about 400 Jewish settlers live in 54 settlement locations among Silwan's 45,000 Palestinian inhabitants.[383] Most of these settlement enclaves have been established by Elad, a private settler organization which, as the operator of the City of David National Park through agreement with the Israel Nature and Parks Authority, acts under color of State authority.[384]

---

378 "The Monthly Report on the Israeli Violations of Palestinian Rights in the Occupied City of Jerusalem," pg. 2. Land Research Center, Arab Studies Society. July 2014.

379 "The Monthly Report on the Israeli Violations of Palestinian Rights in the Occupied City of Jerusalem," pg. 2. Land Research Center, Arab Studies Society. August 2014.

380 al Sanara, 24 September 2014.

381 "Destruction of Palestinian Homes and Heritage in Occupied East Jerusalem: The Case of Silwan," pg. 1. Civic Coalition for Palestinian Rights in Jerusalem.

382 "Number of Jewish Silwan Residents Doubles In Overnight Mission." Haaretez. 20 October 2014.

383 The Case of Silwan, pg. 1.

384 A 2010 lawsuit by Ir Amim, an Israeli NGO, to declare the contract between the Elad and the Nature & Parks Authority declared illegal on the basis of Elad's political agenda and role in settlement activity was dismissed by the Supreme Court of Israel. After the dismissal, Elad and the Authority renewed their contract. See Melanie Lidman, "Court favors right-wing group on City of David park," Jerusalem Post, Mar. 26, 2012, http://www.jpost.com/National-News/Court-favors-right-wing-group-on-City-of-David-park.

2. National Parks

Israel has established two national parks in oEJ: the Jerusalem Walls National Park, which surrounds the Old City, and the Emek Tzurim National Park, on the southern slope of the Mount of Olives. The Jerusalem 2000 Master Plan calls for at least six more national parks in oEJ, three in the final planning stages[385] and three in the early planning stages.[386]

On 27 June 2014, Israel announced construction of one of the national parks in the advanced planning stages: the Mount Scopus Slopes National Park, a national Talmudic garden to be built on 733 dunams of land belonging to the Palestinian oEJ neighborhoods of a-Tur and al-Issawiyeh. The project was approved in November 2013 over the objections of the Environmental Protection Minister, Amir Peretz, whose professional recommendation, as head of the Nature and Parks Authority, concluded that the site is "devoid of particularly sensitive natural elements of value or unique archaeological relics that justify making it a natural park."[387]An Israeli official involved in the plan was caught on tape acknowledging that the park's true purpose is preventing Palestinian construction in the area."[388] On 10 September 2014, Israel's National Planning Committee rejected appeals of Palestinian residents and civil society organizations to halt the park's construction on these grounds.[389]

3. Transportation Infrastructure

From June – September 2014, construction continued on the expansion of the Jerusalem Light Rail (JRL). By connecting Israeli settlements in oEJ with West Jerusalem, the JRL gives effect to an internationally-wrongful act – Israel's purported annexation of East Jerusalem – and facilitates

---

385 These parks are the Mount Scopus Slopes National Park, the Emek Refaim National Park (built on land confiscated from the Palestinian village of Al-Walajeh), and the King's Garden National Park, built on 50 dunams of Silwan's al-Bustan neighborhood.

386 These parks are all located in Palestinian neighborhoods close to the Old City: Bab a-Zahara, Sheikh Jarrah, and the Mount of Olives.

387 B'Tselem, "Mount Scopus Slopes National Park and the harm it causes al-'Esawiyah and a-Tur," Sept. 23, 2014, http://www.btselem.org/jerusalem/national_parks_mount_scopus_slopes.

388 Nir Hasson, "Recording reveals East Jerusalem park is about politics, not environment," Haaretz, Sept. 30, 2013, http://www.haaretz.com/news/diplomacy-defense/.premium-1.549586.

389 Id.

further Jewish settlement in oEJ, in violation of IHL. The JRL seeks to serve civilian, not military, needs and is therefore a clear violation of the law of occupation. Moreover, it largely serves only Jewish areas of the city and settlements in East Jerusalem. For example, only two of the stops on the JLR are in Palestinian neighborhoods, and there has been discussion of trying to reroute the JLR to avoid these areas. In short, the rail was built solely for the benefit of the Jewish residents and settlers of the city.

Additionally, construction of Road 4, a settler-only road project running through the Palestinian community of Beit Safafa, began accelerating rapidly in June 2014. Road 4 will link the Tunnel Road connecting Gush Etzion to Jerusalem in the south, as well as Road 443 in the north. The road ranges from 6-11 lanes and 33-78 meters in width.[390] This road will for the first time establish a contiguous highway between Jerusalem and Jewish settlements in the Bethlehem and Hebron Districts of the West Bank. As such, it is clearly built for the illegal settler population rather than the protected Palestinian population, in violation of international humanitarian law.[391]

The Road 4 project has been condemned by both the UN Human Rights Council and the UN Special Rapporteur on Human Rights in the Occupied Palestinian Territories (OPT). Despite public protests and legal petitions, the residents of Beit Safafa have not found redress in the Israeli courts. In January of 2014, the Israeli Supreme Court sanctioned the completion of the highway notwithstanding the detrimental effect it will have on the Palestinian community.[392] Road 4 will dissect Beit Safafa, detrimentally affecting access, air quality, aesthetics, and property values in the community. There is no benefit to balance these detriments – the highway was designed exclusively to serve the needs of the Jewish settlers, and serve no purpose to the Palestinian residents of Beit Safafa.[393]

---

390 A divided Palestinian neighborhood, torn in two by an Israeli highway." 972mag. 2 March 2013.

391 "Israeli Supreme Court rules to allow completion of the illegal Israeli settlement highway through Beit Safafa, occupied East Jerusalem." Civic Coalition for Palestinian Rights in East Jerusalem. January 2014.

392 "Israeli Supreme Court rules to allow completion of the illegal Israeli Road," 2014. Civic Coalition for Palestinian Rights in Jerusalem, Press Release.

393 "Stop Israeli construction of a new illegal settlement highway in occupied Palestinian territory." Civic Coalition for Palestinian Rights in Jerusalem, Press Release. 6 April 2013.

VIII. Recommendations for Accountability and Reparation

A. "Mowing the Lawn": Maintaining an Illegal Status Quo

This submission has catalogued numerous Israeli violations of IHL and IHRL, placed these violations in their historical and political context, and has demonstrated a pattern of flagrant disregard for the rights of Palestinians in occupied East Jerusalem.

Indeed, the violations occurring during major Israeli military operations in the oPt cannot be understood in a vacuum, but as the product of everyday Israeli policies and practices that violate IHL and IHRL and fuel the chronic outbreaks of violence in the oPt. These policies and practices serve to indefinitely maintain the occupation of Palestine, incorporate the majority of the West Bank territory into Israel, and forcibly transfer the Palestinian population from this territory into enclaves of limited self-rule, thereby disclaiming responsibility for their welfare. Israeli military strategists have described the military offensives to suppress the outbreaks of violence engendered by these policies and practices as "mowing the lawn": routine and periodic acts to maintain an illegal status quo.

B. Relevance of the Goldstone Report

In April 2009, the Human Rights Council commissioned a fact-finding mission on the 2008-2009 Gaza Conflict. This fact-finding mission produced the Goldstone Report, a 430-page investigation into IHL and IHRL violations committed before, during and after the military operations in the Gaza Strip.[394] Sadly, few of the recommendations made in the Goldstone Report have been implemented. Given that little has changed on the ground since those recommendations were made, they remain relevant and imperative. The international community's failure to implement the recommendations of the Goldstone Report contributes to

394 http://www2.ohchr.org/english/bodies/hrcouncil/docs/12session/A-HRC-12-48.pdf

the atmosphere of impunity that surrounds Israel's policies and practices towards Palestinians in the oPt and Palestinian citizens of Israel.

C. Conclusions and Practical Recommendations

Pursuant to the information provided in this report, the Civic Coalition for Palestinian Rights in Jerusalem urges the Independent International Commission of Inquiry to include the following conclusions and recommendations in its report to the 28th Session of the Human Rights Council:

1. Condemnation of Israeli non-cooperation

The Commission should condemn, in the strongest possible terms, the non-cooperation of the State of Israel, which has prevented rapid and first-hand investigation by the Commission of evidence of IHL and IHRL violations in the occupied Gaza Strip and West Bank, including East Jerusalem.

2. Affirming international responsibilities

In light of the documented unwillingness of Israel to carry out impartial and effective domestic investigations, the Palestinian Authority's lack of resources to execute such investigations, and Israel's refusal to cooperate with international investigations such as this Commission of Investigation, the Commission should conclude and affirm that the primary responsibility for the implementation of measures of accountability and reparation lies with the international community, in particular the United Nations.

a. Failure of the UN Security Council to meet its responsibilities

The Commission should express its strong concern about the failure of the Security Council to exercise its responsibilities in connection with the investigation of the serious violations of IHL IHR committed in the context of the 2008-2009 Gaza Conflict (Goldstone Report), including referral of the situation to the International Criminal Court under Article 13(b) of the Rome Statute. Failure of the Security Council to do so has contributed to the continuation of the climate of impunity for these and similar violations, such as those committed since June 2014.

b. Resulting responsibilities of the UN General Assembly and UN member states

In accordance with UNGA Resolution 377A, "Uniting for Peace," should the Security Council fail to exercise its primary responsibility for maintaining international peace and security, it becomes the right and duty of the General Assembly to do so.[395] Given that the Security Council has failed to issue a binding resolution concerning Israel's actions in the oPt on account of the United States veto, the Commission should recommend that the General Assembly adopt resolutions that a) call for an embargo of all military aid to, and cooperation with, Israel and b) ban all trade and cooperation with Israel that contribute to illegal Israeli settlements in the oPt.[396]

The Commission should call on individual states and regional organizations to act independently to support these resolutions by adopting similar measures with regards to their own relations with the Israeli government. The right and responsibility of states to investigate violations of peremptory norms, based on the concept of universal jurisdiction, should also be recognized and the prosecution of such crimes in national courts should be encouraged.

Furthermore, the Commission should express strong concern about evidence suggesting that Israeli violations of IHL and IHRL committed since 13 June 2014 occur in a context of prolonged military occupation with features of apartheid and colonialism, and about incidents of incitement to genocide by Israeli officials and private persons. The Commission should call on the General Assembly to request an advisory opinion from the International Court of Justice on a) the legal consequences of Israel's regime of prolonged occupation that includes elements of colonialism and apartheid, and b) the responsibilities of states and international

395 United Nations General Assembly Resolution 377, commonly known as "Uniting for Peace," http://www.un.org/ga/search/view_doc.asp?symbol=A/RES/377(V).

396 For example, on February 18, 2011, the United States vetoed a draft Security Council resolution condemning all Israeli settlements established in the oPt since 1967 as illegal. The other 14 members of the council voted in favour of the resolution, which was co-sponsored by over 120 States.

organizations to bring to an end the occupation and Israel's settlement activity.

In the interest of providing material support to Palestinian civilians who have suffered injustice and injury as a result of Israel's actions, the Commission should recommend that the General Assembly establish an escrow fund to provide reparations for the loss and/or damage of property and/or persons.

c. Investigation by the International Criminal Court

As of January 2015, the Palestinian Authority has ratified the Rome Statute of the International Criminal Court. This recognition of the Court's jurisdiction over the crimes listed in Article 5 of the Statute allows for the investigation of alleged war crimes, among other crimes, committed in the occupied Palestinian territories. The Commission should recommend to the Prosecutor to start investigation into the IHL and IHRL violations committed in the OPT, including in Gaza and East Jerusalem, since June, and to the State of Palestine to refer the situation to the ICC.

3. Support for the Boycott, Divestment, Sanctions (BDS) Campaign

Article 21 UDHR sets forth the principle that "the will of the people should be the basis of the authority of government," substantiating the principle that the political legitimacy of a state is derived from the consent of its citizens. The state has a responsibility to act in accordance with the expressed will of its citizens. Accordingly, it is the duty of individual citizens to support and strengthen the Boycott, Divestment and Sanctions (BDS) campaign until Israel is held accountable for its violations of international laws and its suppression of the Palestinian people's fundamental rights, including the right to self-determination. Pressure exerted on a government by its citizens has greater potential to alter the course of a state's policies and practices than resolutions and international investigations,. The protection of human rights is a global duty and it is the responsibility of citizens to demand accountability of governments acting on their behalf.

Palestine Works

Palestine Works is a U.S.-based §501(c)(3) nonprofit organization founded in 2012 by diaspora Palestinians to promote Palestinian human rights and human development. Our vision is a Palestinian society that can enjoy the improved prospects and economic, social and political benefits of a strong economy, one powered by the development and deployment of Palestinian human capital. Our mission is to help realize this vision by engaging, developing and harnessing the expertise of young professionals through the creation of high-impact knowledge exchange opportunities, including internships, conferences, publications and networking.

Our projects include the Law Fellowship, which utilizes law students and recent law graduates from around the world to support the work of human rights organizations in Palestine and Israel while developing new advocates for a just, rights-based resolution of the Israeli-Palestinian conflict; and the Young Palestinian Lawyers Fellowship, an intensive program of clinical legal education that builds the capacity of young Palestinian lawyers in occupied Palestine, Israel and the diaspora in public international law, legal writing and oral advocacy while fostering professional development among Palestinian communities.

أشغال لفلسطين
PALESTINEWORKS

palestineworks.org

The Civic Coalition for Palestinian Rights in Jerusalem

CCPRJ was established in 2005 as a coalition of Palestinian civil society organizations that defends the human rights of Palestinians in Jerusalem, and serves Palestinian communities and individuals at risk or affected by Israeli policies that violate international humanitarian and human rights law. Members of the Coalition are Palestinian NGOs and CBOs based inside and outside of occupied East Jerusalem. They work in the fields of development, culture, justice and human rights, and provide support to Palestinian women, children and youth, political prisoners and detainees, and communities affected by forcible displacement.

CCPRJ's executive office is based in East Jerusalem. It coordinates and supports activities of its members and carries out its own program. With this program, CCPRJ promotes issues of common concern, including empowerment of East Jerusalem communities and CBOs, legal aid against dispossession and forcible displacement, protection of East Jerusalem's Palestinian identity and educational institutions, and advocacy for respect of and accountability to international law. CCPRJ conducts research, publishes information materials and submits reports to Palestinian authorities, international aid agencies, foreign mission and the United Nations for this purpose.

civiccoalition-jerusalem.org

Special Thanks

- Ingrid Jaradat-Gassner and Zakaria Odeh, Civic Coalition for Palestinian Rights in Jerusalem.
- Sarah Ihmoud, Ph.D Candidate, Social/Activist Anthropology, University of Texas at Austin
- The CCPRJ field researchers and family members of the victims who contributed to this report, for their courage and conviction.